# Bless This House

BY Anita Bryant

MINE EYES HAVE SEEN THE GLORY
AMAZING GRACE
BLESS THIS HOUSE

# Bless This House

## Anita Bryant

FLEMING H. REVELL COMPANY
OLD TAPPAN, NEW JERSEY

Scripture references in this volume are from the King James Version of the Bible.

"God Bless This House" by Charles Bird, Jr., published by Boban Music Co., Inc. is used by permission.

*Library of Congress Cataloging in Publication Data*

Bryant, Anita.
    Bless this house.

    1. Family—Religious life. I. Title.
BV4526.2.B7        248′.4        72–8409
ISBN 0–8007–0547–5

# *Contents*

# *Foreword*

Never have so many books and pamphlets been written concerning marriage and family life, yet our nation finds itself burdened as never before by the heavy load of broken homes. *This* book is neither a manual, nor a how-to book.

In *Bless This House,* Bob and Anita share with the reader their wonderful Lord, the Builder and Blesser of their home.

> Except the Lord build the house,
> they labor in vain that build it.
> PSALM 127:1

The Green family, in allowing the Lord to be the Builder and Blesser of their home, has the type of home life that is as refreshing as an oasis in a desert.

F. WILLIAM CHAPMAN, Pastor
Northwest Baptist Church
Miami, Florida

# Bless This House

# 1

## Introducing: Bob and Anita Green

*Writing this book, I'm much more Anita Green than I am Anita Bryant. Not that there's any role conflict—Bob Green, my husband, who also heads Bob Green Productions, Inc., Fishers of Men Opportunities, Inc., and is my manager, wouldn't let that happen.*

*The emphasis here, however, will be on our home life. The best role I could possibly play is Anita Green, Bob's wife and our children's mommy. Fortunately, God gave me not only abundant life in the form of a wonderful marriage, but many other opportunities for which I am extremely grateful. He has blessed us beyond measure.*

*Bob and I have been married twelve years. We have four children: Bobby Jr., nine; Gloria Lynn, eight; and Barbara and Billy, our twins, three and one-half. These people represent the heart of my life, and our house is the body around them.*

*Your letters helped "Bless This House" come into being. Three years ago I wrote "Mine Eyes Have Seen the Glory," my autobiographical witness to God's workings in our life. Bob, my husband and best friend as well as spiritual and business partner, naturally became very much a part of that book. Our children entered in, too. The Lord led people from all over America to write to Bob and me—young married couples, grandmothers, preachers, teen-agers, businessmen, even young children. Most shared their problems and Christian testimony with us, and we learned much from these letters.*

*The response was such that, to my surprise, I wrote another book! This one, like the first, definitely had Bob's stamp on it. We are very married. There's just no way to separate our experiences. These particular adventures all tumbled in on our family in six short weeks—and we called the book "Amazing Grace."*

*That was last year. The sharing Bob and I did in "Amazing Grace" led to still more response. Bob hired another secretary to help answer the letters. Many readers wanted specific advice about how to establish a Christian home. Most wanted to hear more from Bob about the male viewpoint. Our publishers suggested we write another book—about marriage and family, this time.*

*But I dawdled around. I just couldn't seem to make up my mind to do it. "The Lord hasn't given me the go-ahead," I told Bob. Bob said that I was lazy.*

Everything began to point Anita and me toward this book. Not just the letters, but the sort of things we heard as we traveled about in the United States. So many people seem to feel family life in our country has become very shaky.

I think families are really searching. I see churches really desperate to get to the young people, using rock music and all kinds of updated gimmicks. The kids may be amused by it—may be temporarily turned on—but it's not lasting.

And that's exactly what they are rebelling against. They want to hear the real thing. They want to know Jesus. Meanwhile, they've been set very bad examples. They've seen a lot of hypocrisy—heard their parents and other adults tell them to do one thing, then seen them go out and do just the opposite.

Families are beginning to see it's time we got back to the Bible and the basic fundamentals—the things Jesus is and the things Jesus taught. It's the slow but sure way. Families are searching for this sureness.

*Bob and I know it's very hard to be a Christian in this day and age. But it's even harder* not *to be a Christian. I no longer can imagine facing any situation without applying Christ to it.*

*This past year, since writing "Amazing Grace," and with the new dimension of witnessing in my life, there's been a heavenly joy. Then there's the contrast between that and the nitty-gritty of life—being a housewife—fixing breakfast and wiping runny noses. It's a comedown, and you wonder, Why can't life be glorious all the time?*

*You have to become mature enough to realize God wants you to bring His spirit to your small children, your cantankerous old husband, and the everyday things of life. That's where it's hardest.*

Sometimes Anita and I get into discussions with families who say, "It's amazing. We never before talked about Jesus with any of our other churchgoing friends. They don't talk about the Bible, Jesus Christ, or any subject like that." And these are nice, moral, well-meaning people!

There's something missing in their lives.

*Bob and I can't feel smug, however. The first years of our marriage were terrible. People who knew us then can see we've changed. They see it and know the difference is Christ. We can't take any credit whatsoever.*

*When Bob bought the prayer altar to surprise me, we all were thrilled with it, but we had absolutely no idea what it would mean to us as a family!*

Right. In our house, we take everything to prayer. Any problem, anybody who gets sick, we pray about it. Bobby prayed one night about his fear of thunder, and he has never been afraid again.

Sometimes Anita and I get cranky and yell at the children. That night at the prayer altar Bobby or Gloria may pray, "Forgive me for my sins. Help me do better in school. And forgive Mommy [or Daddy] for being cranky." When you hear them pray like that you have second thoughts when you're cranky the next time. Then you realize, "Wow, I'm a sinner."

One time Anita got angry at Gloria for something, lost her temper briefly, and spanked Gloria. Gloria cried and Mommy went stalking off. A little later Gloria said to Anita, "Mommy, I forgive you." You have to melt at that point.

We make a point of telling our children that Mommy and Daddy are not perfect, that at times we even may punish them for things they didn't do, or get angry at them when it's not their fault. It is because we're sinners and lose our tempers—and we're far from perfect.

Although we try to set them an example, the only perfect example is Jesus. Don't look to man. Sometimes, we chew the kids out for some small thing and Bobby says, "Well, nobody is perfect." You really have to agree with that!

*Another thing that pointed Bob and me toward this book was the Women's Lib question. In magazine and television interviews, in letters and in person, people keep asking what I think of Women's Lib. I tell them I was liberated when I received Christ as my personal Saviour. That's the only liberation I would ever seek.*

*One of our biggest hang-ups—the reason Bob and I had such a terrible marriage at first—was because I tried to be (as I always had been before marriage) the dominant one. That's my nature. I always preferred to be a leader, not a follower.*

*I'm having to learn the hard lesson of how to follow—not man—but Christ. Of doing things unto Bob, for* Christ's *sake —really doing them as unto Christ, and not caring what reaction I'll get from my husband. Sometimes Bob's reactions aren't particularly Christlike!*

*For me the hardest lesson—I'm trying to learn it as I go along each day—is to become the kind of woman the Bible depicts. I'm thoroughly convinced the other kind of woman is not only warping our children, but ruining America.*

I see nothing wrong in freedom for women, but women have their obligations, too. Anita never has been restricted in any way. Woman's role, as delineated in the Bible, offers all the freedom and genuine liberation any woman could possibly handle.

Man's role is equally well defined by God. He says, among other things, we are to head our households. Someone asked me, "Do you ever have to put your foot down and assert your position as head of the house?"

Every day. Five minutes ago! But I'd never abandon that position, and it's not a phony thing. It's what I feel. It's what I think every man should feel. Too many young men have abandoned that role. They refuse to be heads of their households. It's frightening.

*Also, quite a few young girls these days don't believe in marriage. You almost could get the idea—from them—that a book about marriage and family is old-fashioned!*

Recently Anita and I judged a beauty contest where the girls answered questions about marriage and motherhood. Several said, "I think I'll be a good mother. I plan to stay with my children full-time until nursery school, and then I can go out and work."

Seems as though the girls think it's okay to raise their kids until nursery school, then let others do it from then on. Sure, plenty of husbands want that, too. Some parents ship their kids off to school or to camp all summer just to get rid of them.

Most of the girls we interviewed in this contest said they saw nothing unusual about having sexual intercourse before marriage. These are so-called nice girls, eighteen and nineteen, who without batting an eyelash tell you, "I don't think there's anything wrong with living together before marriage."

You ask why, and discover many come from broken homes. They don't want to make the mistakes their parents made. They'd rather avoid marriage completely.

*These are the kinds of questions that confront Bob and me as we travel across America, speak to young people, and offer our Christian witness in churches and on television. We're not experts on marriage and family life. Our home is not perfect. We don't have all the answers.*

But the Bible does!

*For the sake of ourselves, our children, and our nation, we've got to return to the Bible. A big problem with so-called Christians today is they continually compromise in little ways—until their faith is watered down—with no real power— no power with the children—no discipline—and this is what's wrong with America.*

*However, I'm sick of hearing what's wrong with America. Let's hear more of what's right with America! If we will get back to Almighty God, our nation's Source of strength, in our family and our individual lives, too. . . .*

That's what I told those beauty contestants. I spoke up and said unless our country has a spiritual awakening and a moral revolution, I think we'll go under. We're getting soft. They agreed.

They don't have anybody to look up to. They can't look up to their parents as examples if they're divorced. In society, they can't look up to politics because corruption is widespread. They've not been brought up to believe in Jesus, so they lack that strength. They're stalling along in a day-to-day existence.

These are the young people who soon will be teaching children. They admit they won't be the greatest mothers. They just don't seem to care.

*The optimistic note in all this, however, is that people seem to realize we've got to start at the individual and family level and make a turnabout. It's not easy to do. It's hard work.*

*Sometimes the husband and wife don't think alike about the necessity for God in their household, and this makes problems. But the biggest cop-out in the world is for the wife to blame a family's spiritual apathy on the husband. I know because I've done it myself. It's a great excuse. You can pat yourself on the back to your girl friends, saying, "Isn't it terrible? I want to go church Sunday night, but he wants to watch television."*

*That's a bunch of garbage. I knew I was lying when I said it. There's never been any time Bob didn't allow me to go to church, but there've been times when I used him as an excuse—when I didn't want to go.*

There's quite a story about our churchgoing. Also, there's quite a story behind how Anita decided—very suddenly!—to begin writing this book.

*Bob and I share a marriage, so we'll share this book. He will write some chapters; I will write others. We'll talk about love and marriage, child-rearing, Christian friendships, husband and wife relationships, sex, and taking Christ as a business partner.*

*We also will talk about miracles—the kind that happen when people change, bad situations change, through the grace of God. Bob and I know about these miracles which can happen when you take Christ into your daily life. We know from personal experience how He transforms even a bad marriage—if two people let Him.*

*God's Word is our only authority. The Bible teaches us how to love and discipline a child, guides us as husband to wife, wife to husband, and as to correction, reproof, and instruction. Anything we need can be found in the Bible.*

*My very favorite verse in all Scripture, which I offer you now, is Philippians 4:13, "I can do all things through Christ which strengtheneth me."*

*All of us who feel a tremendous burden for America realize we must start with the individual soul. We must get right with God, get right within the family unit, and begin to trust God for our needs.*

*If we don't turn back to God, I see no way for America to survive. As someone once said, "If God does spare America, He'll have to apologize to Sodom and Gomorrah."*

*We know the importance of our Christian family—and yours. We pray some of our Christian experiences and insights in "Bless This House" somehow will bless your house, too.*

*If so, praise the Lord!*

*Bob Green*

*Anita Bryant Green*

# 2

# Christmas at Villa Verde

I was dreaming of a perfect Christmas—the kind your mind's eye sees so clearly, but which somehow never materializes because your energy just plain runs out. And so does your good behavior.

If *only*, I thought. If *only* we could all get through the holidays with nobody throwing up, or even catching cold. If only I could manage not to get worn-out. If only—miracle of miracles—I could stay perfectly serene and not lose my temper *one single time* during the Christmas season!

Anita, you dreamer. You know yourself. You know who always starts out with such good intentions, then tenses up over nothing. You get overtired, snap at Bob, yell at the kids—just when you crave peace more than anything else in the world.

"Lord, I'm usually the one who throws the monkey wrench into the machinery," I confessed. "This year, please make me different. Give our family some special moments. Don't let me get anxious and caught up in the commercialism of Christmas. Help me love Bob and the children as I should."

Despite that prayer, I really expected the same old thing. But Jesus said, "Ask, and it shall be given you . . ." (Matthew 7:7). So I asked. I really needed something, and God tells us to ask for the things we need. I needed extra, day-to-day grace. Only because I asked for it (I now realize) were we able to put Christ in our family's Christmas.

Actually, in retrospect, I see the process began months earlier when I quit blaming Bob for all the times our family failed. That's right. I could actually be that unfair!

Sometimes I resented Bob because things weren't perfect in our family. I blamed him—he was my scapegoat. It's the one you love most—the one closest to you—that you push the blame on when you don't want to face up to yourself.

I wanted Bob to be the spiritual head of our family. Yet what held him back, as I had to realize, was my own ineffectiveness as a Christian in our home!

Ironically enough, for most of our married life Bob has urged me to give my Christian witness publicly. He'd push me into a corner. Because of him I've spoken to countless thousands of people at the Billy Graham Crusades, on the Oral Roberts television specials, at prayer breakfasts, churches, and all sorts of places. It was Bob with Bruce Howe at Word Records who encouraged me to record sacred songs; and it was Bob, together with Dick Shack of the Agency for the Performing Arts, who helped persuade me to write *Mine Eyes Have Seen the Glory* to testify to what Jesus has done in our lives.

In *Amazing Grace,* I told of leading Mary Hendrick, the

twins' nursemaid, to the Lord. Her salvation blessed our entire household, but especially me, because outlining to Mary the simple steps required to walk the life of faith suddenly forced me to recognize my own failings.

I didn't like what I saw. *At home, my Christian witness simply didn't hold up.*

I really had to come to terms with myself. What good is it just to witness to others about your salvation, I asked myself, if it doesn't show at home? To apply God's love in a Spirit-filled daily walk with Him effectively, offer Him your relationship with husband and children and let Jesus guide in the nitty-gritty and the little things. Here is where it counts.

Truthfully, I could hardly even confess those particular sins to myself—much less turn them over to the Lord. The truth hurt. It hurt to realize how many of our family's problems were of *my* making. I had been really blind to that.

I saw I had been angry with Bob for offering criticism and for simply speaking the truth on occasion. Meanwhile I had become increasingly critical of *him*—particularly his spiritual side which I continually cut down. This cutting-down process held him back in his Christian growth. That made him seem (to me) all the more obstinate. In short, I blamed Bob for any lack of love in our home—yet my carping criticisms and my nagging were killing some of his love!

This sort of situation builds up over a period of time, and it takes time to correct. When God gives you the first of a series of such devastating insights into yourself (He's too loving and kind to dump the whole load on you at once, lest you go out of your mind!) there's only one place to go—to Him. On your knees, you become as a little child. You get back to basics. In that struggle, often with tears of remorse, you begin to learn new things about God's love and patience and forgiveness, and you ask Him to supply you with these gifts to apply to your husband and children.

For me, the task often seemed nearly impossible. My nature doesn't yield easily, and at first my failings seemed to multiply rather than diminish. One of the devil's favorite tools is discouragement, I've learned, and sometimes he uses it with me very effectively.

Two things helped enormously in my battle with Satan. One was a magnificent passage of Scripture which I commend to you—Luke 11:9–13. In these verses Jesus tells us exactly how to attain anything we need. He spells out what we're to do, and it's all very plain. I claimed that Scripture and followed it to the letter.

In addition, I learned to turn to God first thing in the morning. Go to Him early with your love and praise, your needs and problems. If you start the day without that communion with Him, before you know it, the day takes you over. Then a couple of days may go by before you even have room in your life for God.

You need that quiet time with Him, in a closet, by your bed, or wherever. You need to start off the day with Him. Otherwise the devil gets in and maneuvers things so you don't get the time, and you may go several days without fellowship with your Father. There hasn't been that daily grace applied to your routine. That grace comes only with humbling yourself before your Father and asking Him for it, because you certainly can't conjure it up yourself.

It came as a shock to me that God wanted me to start with the little things and quit worrying about the weeks ahead. Just to stop worrying about tomorrow and let God take care of today has been the hardest thing I've ever tried to do.

Big hurdles don't throw me nearly so hard because I expect God to take care of them. But when I don't take time to ask God to help with my small needs, the devil always steps in. Too many Christians don't take time to ask because we don't think God wants to be bothered with "little things." That's a spiritual trap. I've come to see this is exactly where God wants us to begin.

Such things as disciplining the children when you're overly tired—being able to listen with love and understanding to the older ones when they come home from school; to show real interest in your husband when you're worn-out from the children—these are vitally important!

Slowly (with much struggle), I learned to give the so-called small problems to the Lord. We can't conquer such obstacles, but the Christ in us can. That way we grow on a strong foundation. If we do fail, it's from the top (which can be rebuilt) and not from a crack in the foundation of our faith.

Then came Christmas. I knew it would be a faith-testing time because for me it's the season to be uptight. My mind whirled with cooking, shopping, wrapping, entertaining, and all the other things to do. Also, immediately after the holiday would come important professional commitments. We'd have the Orange Bowl Parade to commentate for the fifth consecutive year, plus the Junior Parade, as well as the halftime show at the Orange Bowl football game. Also, I'd agreed to sing the national anthem at a football game between our Miami Dolphins and the Baltimore Colts. I could foresee a tough, hectic time.

Christmas. Professional bookings. It couldn't all be done—not well, that is—and I knew it. What a shame to downgrade Christmas for any reason! So I took these feelings, along with my usual problems, to God.

We go all out at Christmas, Lord. Bob is Swedish and I'm old-fashioned and sentimental, and we spread Christmas all through the house. We really love our live, twelve-foot Christmas tree, tall enough to touch the ceiling. We cherish the ornaments from Sweden and everywhere in the world we've traveled. Our tree, glorious in the center of our living room, seems to us the most beautiful one in the world.

But Father, these physical preparations are nothing unless we can show our children the love and joy and peace of Jesus Christ. Please help us remember this.

We began four Sundays before Christmas day.

"This is the beginning of *Advent,* and *advent* means *coming,*" we told the children. "Jesus is coming. This is a special time to prepare our hearts for the Baby Jesus."

Edith Beers (Mrs. William Beers of Atlanta) sent us a very lovely Advent tree. We placed this on a coffee table in the living room. Each night after dinner we'd hang another tiny gift on the Advent tree, while Bob took time to read the story of the tree (which Edith wrote) and discuss how we were waiting for Christ.

The children loved it, of course, and Bob and I did, too. It's fun to count off the days until Christmas. Best of all, it put the emphasis where it belongs—on Jesus instead of Santa Claus.

The Advent season helps keep Christmas holy. This was the first time we'd celebrated Advent which is widely observed by Christians of all denominations over most of the world. For some reason it never quite caught on in America until recent years, but it's spreading—and it's a custom more of us ought to adopt.

Each family discovers its own ways of celebrating Christmas. Certain things—ornaments handed down from childhood, perhaps an annual open house, little family customs—become very precious. Two things in particular, both passed down from grandparents, enhance Christmas for us.

One came from Bob's father, Einar Green. Farfar, as the children call him (*Farfar* means "father's father" in Swedish), carved a handsome, tall wooden candelabra which holds five candles. He might be surprised to know how much we treasure this because he made it with his hands. How many other men have such talented fingers?

The other favorite thing came from my Grandma Berry, so it means a lot to me. It's simply a recipe for candy, Grandma Berry's Chocolate Toes, but it holds all kinds of memories for me.

Grandma couldn't afford to buy presents for all her grandchildren and great-grandchildren, so she made these chocolate toes as a love token. Back then, if you found real nuts and an orange in your stocking, that was a treasure. We kids appreciated these candies not only because they were delicious, but because Grandma made them herself. We loved them the most of all our Christmas presents.

Sometimes Grandma let me help her make them. It's easy. You take a box of 10-X powdered sugar, ¼ pound of sweet butter, and work these together with your fingers until the mixture becomes flaky and can be worked into a ball. Pinch off small pieces and shape them like brazil nuts. Melt one slab of paraffin (there are two in a box) with four squares of unsweetened chocolate. Cool. Dip candy into the coating until it's thoroughly coated and place on waxed paper to dry.

This is something almost any age can do. Some days after school the older kids and I spent the afternoon making Chocolate Toes and peanut brittle from Grandma's recipes. We really enjoyed working together, and it seemed like an unexpected dividend of the Christmas season—the closeness I'd prayed for.

One day we were making Chocolate Toes, and Bobby and Gloria were shaping the candies, when I received a long-distance phone call. I knew it would tie me up a little while.

"Don't worry, Mommy, I can do it," Gloria assured me.

"If you have any trouble, call Daddy," I said.

When I returned she had finished making all that candy—and it was done perfectly. It was one of those sharp, magic moments that stay in your mind. I took a good look at Gloria, the little mother. *My daughter is growing up. She can handle things.* It was as though I saw her for the first time as a little adult, no longer completely a child.

Moments like that are so precious. I saw Gloria differently, and throughout the Christmas season God continued to give me that sort of blessing—a new *awareness.*

During the holidays, it was as if I were outside of myself, looking at different people and enjoying them. These were times I could keep forever, like snapshots you could paste in an album.

There was our party for the Miami Dolphins, which is becoming an annual custom. Bob is a football nut, so naturally he's crazy about the Dolphins. At first I admit I didn't completely share his enthusiasm. My philosophy about football was about as practical as that of most wives. If you can't lick 'em, join 'em. So I just went along with Bob on football—at first.

Now I'm becoming a football nut myself because we've met some of our finest Christian friends among the Dolphins and their wives. Our Christmas party was like a fellowship. Brother Bill Chapman, our pastor, talked after dinner. It was such a sweet, sharing time. We had a beautiful evening.

Jesus said, "Ask, and it shall be given to you." And the

blessings continued to come. Uncle Luther Berry and Aunt Marie spent their vacation in Miami over Christmas. Uncle Luther is a Baptist minister, as is his son Renny, who had become associate pastor of a Miami church.

This was the first time I'd seen Uncle Luther and Aunt Marie since Grandma Berry's funeral, when the sermon he preached over his mother's grave made such a soul-stirring, unforgettable testimony to the power of Christian life.

We were able to show Uncle Luther and Aunt Marie a fantastic time. They went with us to the Orange Bowl Parade. We got tickets for the Orange Bowl football game, and also the Miami Dolphins-Baltimore Colts game.

We also had them to Christmas Eve dinner. Renny and his wife Janet were with us, as were Farmor and Farfar Green, and Jody Dunton, who became our friend during those dark days when she, with other staffers at Jackson Memorial Hospital, battled to save our newborn, dying, premature twins. Now those lively, funny twins, with their big brother and sister, were digging in to a big turkey dinner.

Suddenly grateful for each precious face at our table, I felt overwhelmed to realize how God had transformed Christmas for us. Dinner wasn't hectic at all. We felt conscious of closeness, of family, of love—and God had given me an extra measure of grace and serenity.

There was such love at the table I just wanted to linger there. Then Bob led the way to the music room, Janet played the piano, and we all sang carols. You could feel the Holy Spirit among us, then and later, as we exchanged presents around the tree. I hold it all in my heart, a clear picture of one of the most wonderful family evenings we ever spent.

There are other holiday "snapshots," some really surprising.

"You're so much nicer this Christmas than before,

Mommy," Bobby confided. "I see a big difference." It was a blunt compliment but nevertheless appreciated.

"I prayed for that, Bobby," I told him.

At one point during Christmas I gave my testimony and sang to my Sunday-school department at Northwest Baptist Church. "I asked the Lord to show me 'Peace, be still,' " I told them. "I really prayed for that specific thing, and He heard. There's been such a big difference in our household— one even our children comment on."

Charlotte Topping and Marabel Morgan were there. Suddenly I felt their special love and sisterhood so strongly it became hard to speak. I cried as I finished my simple testimony.

"If we could get back to putting Jesus in Christmas, if we could put our eyes on Him instead of on the tinsel . . . .

"When He's in our heart, He wants us to share with others. Our greatest gift is to give God's gift—Jesus Christ— to others." Knowing Charlotte had been my special gift this year, for I had helped lead her to the Lord—and Marabel had prayed for us every step of the way. Looking into their faces that morning, I felt overwhelmed by love and a sense of God's amazing grace.

I'm thinking of the Christmas star Bob and Pedro Vasquez (Pedro assists with the house and grounds, our boat, and anything else that needs skill) erected at the front of Villa Verde. Bob had Pedro construct the star, six feet high, outlined in lights. At the rear of the house, overlooking Bay Biscayne, Pedro's twelve-foot lighted cross gleams across the waters.

Pedro built the cross and the star and built them well. They touch my heart and remind me of Matthew 5:16; "Let your light so shine before men, that they may see your good works, and glorify your Father which is in heaven." As the star and the cross shine out into our soft Miami night, carrying a message of God's love to all who see them, God places a thought in my mind. "It's well to light our home on the outside. We must take care to let Jesus light it inside."

The Christmas star. The cross of Christ. I wish these lights may shine everywhere in the world, into each home and each heart. I pray their glow reaches your house, too.

# 3

*Bob Green*

# Life with Anita

What's it like, being married to a star? That question always catches me off-balance. I never know how to answer it.

You see, Anita Bryant is essentially a wife and a mother. I really don't think of her as a star. She is my wife. The career is there, of course. We're both involved in it, but her career is separate from *us*. There are several other facets of Anita far more important to me than her talent and success.

We started out as any other couple—just romantically in love. Both of us were in show business at the time we met. I was pretty well established as a disc jockey for radio station WINZ in Miami. She was a vivacious nineteen-year-old beauty who had been second runner-up in the Miss America pageant, a pop singer who already had a gold record (which represents one million sales) to her credit.

I fell hard for Anita. In Genesis 2:18 it says, "And the

Lord God said, It is not good that the man should be alone; I will make him an help meet for him." I certainly wasn't thinking in Biblical terms then because I was not yet a born-again Christian. But I was ready to get married!

When you live with someone, the glamor edge wears off. You're looking at a wife and a mother and something entirely different from mere glamor. Consequently, I don't think of Anita as glamorous. I just don't think of her in those terms. I think of her as fun. She's so many people rolled up into one. I like that.

We have a relationship on many levels: Christian, family, business, witnessing, and we're also great friends and lovers. That's fortunate, since we're together almost 100 percent of the time. We're almost never separated.

Anita and I share most of the same desires and goals. We're both homebodies. We could have had great problems if one of us had wanted to stay on the road all the time—if we had put career first. Fortunately, each of us has the same primary interests: our children, family, and home.

Our first year or two of marriage was a real power struggle. I was not filled spiritually at the beginning of our life together, and this must have caused great frustrations within Anita.

Also, we were both immature. Had I known God then, our marriage would have been very different. I could have taken the lead in our home and could have influenced her. As it was, she was a good Christian who had no leadership at home. I pulled her down to my level.

Before I became Spirit-filled, Anita suspected her career mattered more to me than anything else. She has changed. She now realizes I don't put anything ahead of our home life.

My desires are very simple. Family is all that's important to me outside of my faith. I'm not typical, I suppose. I think these home-centered ideas are a result of my upbringing. My parents, Einar and Svea Green, came from Sweden. Americans born of European parents seem to have stronger family ties.

The more generations away from the mother country, the less important the family unit in America seems to become. Our family consisted of the three of us, and we were very close. The Jewish fellows I grew up with in the Bronx, New York, also had close ties to Europe, and their families, like mine, were strong.

I think it's important to delineate the differences in family members' traits, attitudes, and functions. Females are able to endure pain and childbirth, for example, and they reach different emotional peaks from anything males ever know. I love my children as much as Anita does. Maybe I'm more demonstrative with my children than other men are with theirs, but I don't have that motherly instinct—whatever it is—that gives her more patience with the children.

I could never take on a mother's duties. Nor does Anita really want my role as head of the household. Nevertheless there are times, and I suppose this happens with most women, when her bossiness does come out.

At those times, when temperament rears its head, I have a choice. I can say to myself, "Forget it, you're still running the house," or I can back down. I can see how problems are created in a household where the husband takes the easy way, and cops out. Over the years the negative effects of such a course would prove disastrous.

If you have to think of this "head of the house" bit too much, it's not coming naturally—and there's something wrong. If you have to sit down and say, "Today I didn't really act like I'm head of the house. Tomorrow I'd better apply myself," then I think you're in bad shape.

It's got to be natural. Sometimes, however, the male takes the path of least resistance. The easy way out is to say, "Wow, I've gotta get away from her and the kids. I'd better get out with the guys, or play a game of golf, and just escape." The Lord knows there are plenty of escapes in the world. A man can always get away from the house. But is that a cop-out?

I'm an incurable homebody. Anita has to take me or leave me, in that respect. I just want to stay home all the time. I love the family and love the house and everything that goes with all that. I just want to stay home with the kids on Saturday mornings, just having them around and being around them. I'm pretty lucky.

I don't think every man feels that way, and I'm not saying I'm better than others because I do. That just happens to be me. Because of this trait in me, and because Anita and I always travel together, we're forced to be together at times when maybe we'd prefer not to be. We're much more together than most couples are. This brings tensions sometimes.

How do we deal with tensions? The human way, a lot of the time. We fight, yell at each other, and make up. Oh, nothing violent, nothing out of the ordinary. We disagree loudly sometimes, and that's it.

Trouble is, I have a hot temper—especially when I'm dieting. Anita also has a quick temper. That's a combination like gasoline and matches. I seethe and stew and keep things inside and too often resort to sarcasm which really hurts Anita.

My wife and I are not afraid to fight. We have our battles and confrontations like other couples. Anita has a hot temper and lets it all out, while I brood, which is a potentially dangerous combination. We have to learn how to accept one another, or our marriage could be just plain awful.

Over the years, we've learned a few things about ourselves. We now know it's not the argument, but the aftermath that matters. You have to take it to prayer. You realize these unlovely sides of your nature are the traits of sinners. No hassle in the world is really all that important. It's the people who matter more than anything else.

It's such sins of the flesh as a hot temper, or pride, that usually throws Anita or me. When pure malice flashes out occasionally, we believe that's the devil at work. We talk to the children about that. They realize the devil sometimes can get hold of their parents, of them, or of anybody else.

You'll often hear Anita and me quote Brother Bill Chapman, our pastor at Northwest Baptist Church in Miami. Brother Bill and Peggy, his wife, don't just preach Christian marriage, but live it before you. Their partnership is a beautiful thing.

Brother Bill often says, "When you see the devil coming—*run!*" That's good advice. You can get to a point where you can avoid many problems by seeing them up ahead—and sidestepping.

Anita and I confess our sins alone, or with the family at the altar. Every fight we have brings the combatants back to God, humbly, as we confess, "I'm a sinner. Help me fight off those times the devil takes me over."

If you recognize your sins and confess them and continually pray, God will help you work out these problems. I've cut down on shouting at the children—not that I really lost my temper and yelled at them a lot—but I do it even less now because just before my anger causes me to raise my voice or give them a smack, I say a quick prayer.

At that point you say to yourself, "I'm not perfect. They're not perfect." And somehow you're not yelling at them but you're able to reason with them. You have to make up your mind the kind of father you want to be.

I have constantly in the back of my mind that they grow up so fast. I've seen so many tragic examples of where parents—particularly fathers—fall out of fellowship with their children, and suddenly the kids start having problems. Then the father realizes he must shape up and spend more time with his children, but by then it's too late.

The formative years start immediately. I don't want to lose any of my time with my kids because I can't get that time back.

I'm a father to my children, not a pal. I assert my authority. I spank them at times, and they respect me for it. Sometimes I take Bobby into the music room, and it's not so I can play him a piece on the piano. We play a piece on the seat of his pants!

I have fellowship with them after they're spanked. I explain before the spanking why they must be punished, and make sure they understand. They don't like it but they know they deserve it. In Proverbs 13:24 we're told, "He that spareth his rod hateth his son: but he that loveth him chasteneth him [early]." That's strong stuff—the idea that a father who won't spank actually *hates* his child.

Anita and I have found that if you're able to pray about it, physical spankings assume the proper perspective. They're necessary at times, and the Bible instructs us to chasten our wayward or rebellious children, but they're not the *only* way to reach a child. And always—*always*—they must be administered in love.

A man must set a Christian example for his family, and this never will be easy. The only effective means toward self-control I know of is prayer. Anita and I do much more praying these days than we used to do. We take our marital frictions to the Lord in prayer, and our child-rearing problems, too.

We need to be realistic about ourselves and one another. Anita has certain hang-ups. I have certain hang-ups. Some we'll be able to shake, others we won't. In the back of my mind I desperately hope that if I don't get rid of all that stuff, at least I won't pass it on to my children.

Meanwhile, I discover that as I grow older I soften in some ways. I compromise more, overlook the less important items. I think that happens in every marriage. In the early days you feel you have to prove everything.

I no longer care to argue every point. I believe in reasoning together on all points that really matter. What happens in too many homes, however, is that the husband gradually weakens and habitually takes the easy way out—eventually relinquishing all decisions to his wife. That's death to a marriage.

The greatest strengths within our marriage center around a common religious basis. Until a few years ago, prayer never entered my life. I never prayed about things. We wouldn't go back to our old way of life. People ask me if the Christian life isn't hard—a lot of trouble to be loyal to—yet these same people don't find it difficult to be loyal to a ball team, or go bowling on a regular basis.

Little by little we're finding a good balance in our life— fun and friendships, worship and witness, work and play—and it gets better all the time.

Life with Anita is not glamorous but it's real. She's not perfect and neither am I, but she's always interesting. You never know what may happen next with her!

I'll tell you a little story to illustrate that. First, however, let me say one thing. Throughout this book, Anita and I share our scraps, our disagreements, our failures, because these too are part of our lives. But let me emphasize that for us, relatively new to the Christian way of marriage, the times of happiness, victory, and fun far outweigh all the other times.

People often comment that we seem to have an extremely happy family life. Our children are obedient, cooperative, and responsible people most of the time. I have a lovely wife and I'm a lucky man—but we're still human, and we do spat. Recently we'd had a tiff and Anita was nasty to me. We were flying to an engagement somewhere, and we weren't speaking. I hadn't prayed about it, either. I wasn't ready to pray about it.

Since we weren't speaking, Anita wrote me this little note:

## To My Husband Bob

I'll try to be a wife to you
The way the Bible tells,
Then maybe God will say to me,
"My child, you've served Me well!"
Your trying wife,
ANITA

What can you do? Anyhow, as I said before, there's never a dull moment for the man married to Anita Bryant!

# 4

# Lord, Teach Me to Submit

"Know how you can tell if somebody's really a Christian? Go home with him!"

Brother Bill's humor really hits home. As self-conscious laughter rippled around the room, I silently agreed. *Yes. Talk to the husband and children.*

So much I read, heard, and studied those days led straight to a road marked WITNESS AT HOME. It amounted to a continuous challenge. Our home appeared to be a normal, happy, Christian place. Bob and I had no exceptional amounts of friction—only occasional blowups, which by day's end always seemed to smooth out okay.

". . . let not the sun go down upon your wrath" (Ephesians 5:26) is something Bob and I heed. We don't often harbor a grudge; both forgive easily. We had no serious problems, I supposed. It was more a desire to perfect our day-to-day walk with Christ.

Marabel Morgan increased that desire in me as she talked about her course entitled "The Total Woman." Marabel not only is my darling friend and Christian sister, but also my prayer buddy. She based her course on the Bible, and I like the subtitle: "How to Make Your Husband Adore You."

Marabel researches continually, and shares her discoveries with me. Her enthusiasm is so con†agious, so upbeat and optimistic, I just knew all that womanliness was bound to rub off on me. Much as I kidded her, however—and I kid Marabel unmercifully—at the same time, I knew God was dealing with me in those very same areas of my life. And Marabel, naturally, is one of His instruments.

So I prayed and studied the Bible a great deal, and God gave me one amazing insight after another—a series of personal revelations about my needs and failings as a woman, a wife, and a mother.

To add even further impetus to my desire to grow, Brother Bill began teaching the New Members Class lessons—Bible-based, of course—expounding what Christ expects of wives, husbands, parents, and children. Sometimes God just seems to bombard you from all sides!

All this began to change my heart. I became convinced women must study the Bible in order to learn how God wants us to live. That's the only way we'll ever find real fulfillment as females.

An enormous problem in America today—and it's man's fault as well as woman's—is our sinfulness against God as each of us individually persists in carving out his own personal set of rules, his own so-called rights. This is no small matter. I've come to believe America ultimately will be endangered unless each of us endeavors to become a really strong, godly man or woman.

Many who profess and call themselves Christians absolutely flinch at God's requirements for full manhood and womanhood. For example, consider Ephesians 5:22–24:

> Wives, submit yourselves unto your own husbands, as unto the Lord.
> For the husband is the head of the wife, even as Christ is the head of the church: and he is the saviour of the body.
> Therefore as the church is subject unto Christ, so let the wives be to their own husbands in every thing.

How much plainer could it be stated? I thought I'd never describe myself as submissive. But *submissive,* I was to learn, doesn't mean *timid.* It doesn't mean a woman is meant to be overrun, downtrodden, and all that. To submit is a voluntary act of love and trust. It's a deliberate yielding and deferring to your husband, in obedience to God's plan for your life. Until we do that, we can't please God.

Think of today's unhappy women who struggle to usurp men's authority. Their efforts can only be fruitless and result in self-defeat and misery because I can't see where they're supported by God's Word.

Though most of us women don't consider ourselves activists in that sort of struggle, we may actually end up in the same camp—if we nag, bicker, criticize, and undercut the man God gave us to love, rather than submitting our lives and hearts in perfect trust and support.

Marabel's life dramatically illustrates what I mean. In fact, her resolution to stop nagging Charlie Morgan led to her researching and developing her own wife-to-husband approach. These eventually evolved into her Total Woman classes which became tremendously successful here in Miami Beach.

See if her story parallels yours in any way. It really hit home with me!

Charlie and I loved one another, but he never talked to me. We were "happily married." Anybody would say so. But why was I so uptight? I'd always pictured myself as a serene, loving woman who never got cross with her husband or children. Meanwhile, Charlie often said, "Gee, you sure come unglued easily, don't you?"

One day I realized I *nagged* Charlie. I constantly tried to remake him. I was always telling him small things I disliked about him—things he ought to improve. I saw he had begun to crawl into a shell. He had begun to think of me as a second mother. I could see *I* was the one cutting down the flame of our romance.

That day Marabel made a drastic decision:

I promised myself I'd never nag Charlie Morgan again. That night I told my husband I'd never nag him again but was going to accept him *exactly as he was.* I'm certain he didn't believe me. I stuck to it, however. From that day to this, our lives, our marriage, and everything else has become fantastically better.

There's much, much more to Marabel's amazing story. In her very first lesson she makes an extremely significant point, and reiterates it often: "You must accept your husband as he is. The reason you can is that God loves you and accepts you just as you are!"

That's exactly the principle God showed me. I realized I must stop criticizing Bob's lack of spiritual development and work only on my own. I could see my carping literally undercut my husband's confidence, desire, and ability to grow in Christ. Of course I mentally defended that nagging as something I had to do for Bob's good, but that's because I didn't know the Bible very well.

I'd never try to get away with that now. The Bible doesn't uphold a nagging wife *anywhere*—and Bob knows it. The devil can disrupt many a would-be Christian household via the woman's tongue. Unfortunately, he's done some damage this way at Villa Verde. Nagging, anger, criticism, sharp remarks, negative ideas—oh, that tongue is as a sharp-edged sword!

In Ephesians (such a rich book!) Paul speaks directly to that. In chapter 4, verses 31 and 32, he says:

> Let all bitterness, and wrath, and anger, and clamour, and evil speaking, be put away from you, with all malice:
> And be ye kind one to another, tenderhearted, forgiving one another, even as God for Christ's sake hath forgiven you.

What if a wife truly lacks confidence in her husband? Perhaps he's critical of her, hard to please, unfair. Should she submit to that kind of man? The Bible says she should. The inference is plain: Live out your Christian life before Him so that you influence your partner for the good. God says that's a woman's responsibility.

Husbands can disappoint wives for many reasons and in many ways. Some women, especially those who lost their fathers in childhood due to death or divorce, really want a daddy more than a husband. Their search for lost childhood robs the husband. (After all, how can he meet the needs a father should have supplied—needs and dissatisfactions a woman probably isn't conscious of having and can't even express in words?)

Perhaps I've expected Bob to be Daddy. I don't know. My parents divorced when I was thirteen, and as so many girls do, I did miss my father.

Submission, in the Biblical meaning of the word, becomes the only answer to that sort of problem. "Looking up to" the man as head of the house constantly asserts and reaffirms him. As I can support him with faith and trust, he can protect and complete me.

Husbands don't come readymade, all packaged and prepared. Neither do wives. But as soon as one of them—either one—begins to follow the marital precepts outlined in the Bible, the other will desire to comply. That is, compliance follows where the first partner acts in love, as God would wish, rather than strict, joyless legalism.

Duty is stern; love is winsome. The loving wife always has more fun in marriage because God planned it that way. He really does provide us with joy and abundant life if we'll just follow His blueprints.

When we as wives decide to submit to the man we love, that means we're truly willing to change our natures. First, we need insight as to the places in life and marriage where we don't meet God's criteria. By reading the Bible we discover where these places are. Then we must learn, through reading the Word, how to overcome—which only can be done by the grace of God, diligent prayer, and faithfulness.

You'll find your prototype in the Bible, I discovered; not only the kind of person you are, but a description of your feelings, your condition, and how to deal with it. It's all there. If you're faithful about reading and praying about it, the Word will reveal what you need in your life.

In Sunday school we studied the four natures Christians display. I think mine is sanguine, like Peter's. In Matthew 26:33, he shows a quick display of emotion and is so outspoken and impetuous. I really identify with Peter!

Then there's the phlegmatic nature, the ho-hum sort of person who often follows the line of least resistance. This is described in 1 Timothy 4:14–16.

The Apostle Paul, as depicted in 2 Timothy 4:7 exemplifies the choleric nature; a strong, determined, bulldog sort of person.

The melancholy nature, as in 1 John 3:16–18, represents loyalty and love. This is a fragile spirit which easily can be offended. I identify with that, too. I can see something of myself in all these natures—especially Peter's.

Study the Bible enough, and I'm convinced you can become your own analyst. Jesus Christ is the perfect psychiatrist. By applying the Word of God to my life, knowing I'm born again, being lifted from sins through the blood of Christ, I see I can be delivered from the power of Satan, through Jesus. Miracles are possible. And sometimes, in any marriage, it takes a miracle.

People in the world can see this change. They comment that you're different, that your personality is emerging. They recognize your changed life, but don't know it's the Christ in you.

God has had to show me that after my finding the joy of Christian life, and after He started me digging in the Word, He would continue to point out areas which need changing. Challenge follows challenge. There's a Scripture text, Philippians 1:6, which speaks to that.

The woman who seriously intends to follow Jesus really desires to submit to her Lord. She knows that's the only way. She desires this because she loves Him.

Only as I practice yielding to Jesus can I learn to submit, as the Bible instructs me, to the loving leadership of my husband. Only the power of Christ can enable a woman like me to become submissive in the Lord.

Christ becomes the means, then, toward perfecting and sanctifying a woman's cherished relationship to her man. In this way He fuses the two of them and creates a Christian marriage.

# 5

# *Sunday Morning Battles*

I had become a Sunday morning tyrant.

The devil seemed to work overtime on me that day, and it was demoralizing our family. Going to church (of all things!) was the problem. I knew it was our duty to go, and I yearned to go, but there certainly was no joy.

Those mornings were terrible. Sunday school begins at 9:15, and Bob wasn't happy to go. He realized from the beginning that Sunday would be a dreadful day.

Bob got so he hated Sunday mornings. So did I (with breakfast to cook and four kids to dress) and if anyone got off schedule or anything went wrong, I was yelling at them.

I'd jump right out of bed and whirl into action—whiz down and start breakfast, yell up at the kids, try to get them out of bed and *started*—and Bob would come trailing down later. He was in no hurry. He was as slow as the rest of them.

When I admitted it was at home that my Christian

51

challenge was most difficult, I knew our Sundays would never make it in the Lord's sight. My heart sank just thinking about it.

The very day I should have had extra love, compassion, and understanding for my family, I was yelling more than ever at the kids—and hardly speaking to Bob.

Obviously *I* was the key. I got the whole day off to a bad start. Later I'd blame Bob. "You really don't want to go to church at all," I'd say. He'd usually give me a disgusted look and not even bother to answer.

Because we had to scramble so to get to church, it didn't occur to me to begin the day with prayer. Instead I'd jump right out of bed without taking time to get on my knees to ask God to give me grace. That was my first mistake.

Then I'd run down and start breakfast. I'd yell at the kids three or four times, trying to get them up, and Bob dragged himself out of bed even later. Then I'd dash back up to get myself dressed. By this time everybody was in a foul mood.

Once we finally piled into the car I'd start nagging Bob about going to church that night. That was horrible timing on my part because of course he didn't want to go. It was such a rat race—such a hectic thing—to make it even on Sunday morning!

So I'd sit in the car fussing at Bob, putting on my earrings, putting on lipstick, brushing my eyebrows. The babies would be crying in the back, Bobby and Gloria fighting, and I'd pick on Bob: "You didn't do this," or, "You didn't do that!" We'd have a miserable ride to church. By the time we got there I'd have straightened the kids out, and somehow managed to put a smile on my face.

Later Bob would say, "Soon as we get to church you get all goody-goody. You want to hold my hand and act lovey-dovey. What about on the way to church? When we get up in the morning? Why can't you be nice then?"

He kept repeating this to me. I didn't like hearing it because it was true. My actions were providing a negative testimony to Bob who has looked up to me as a Christian. I came to the Lord at age eight, while Bob was saved the night before our wedding. Bob thought of me as a strong Christian, but these flaps discouraged him. He was becoming really disillusioned. He just couldn't understand why I couldn't overcome these apparently small things, and why I wasn't a happier person.

The Holy Spirit showed me those Sunday mornings resulted from my own wretchedness. At first I didn't even talk to Bob about it. I felt it had to be between Christ and myself. Bob was aware of my problems but he couldn't help me.

God showed me I had to stop dumping all the blame on Bob. If I were to set him any sort of Christian example, I must somehow show love, calmness, patience, all those things, *before* I went to Sunday school.

At home is where it really counts. It wasn't just a matter of going to church and hearing the Word, allowing the Holy Spirit to come into your heart and convict you of your sins. True, the rest of the day can go all right after that. But the walk with God needs to start even before church does, and it should be a continuous thing.

So Christ brought me to terms with myself and made me face facts. When I first started witnessing, particularly after leading Charlotte Topping to the Lord, I'd experienced a marvelous kind of Christian joy. I began to realize I'd been missing that joy all those years, that I did so many things out of mere habit, in obedience to God—and *still* missed the real point of Christianity.

Until you realize God wants to take over every facet of your life, wants you to be faithful not just in going to Sunday school and church, but also faithful to Him in your attitudes at home—well, I had sinned much.

I resolved to change our Sunday mornings by changing myself. I knew good resolutions wouldn't do it. I'd tried and failed too many times in the past.

I'd usually take a problem of this type to the family altar, confess my sins to God before my family, and they'd pray about it, too. This time I didn't do it that way.

Instead I silently turned it over to the Lord. I told Him I just couldn't do a thing about Sundays at our house, but *He* could. Christ's promises are in His Word, and I knew He could and would help me.

Things immediately began to change—as I expected. When I began yielding each day to Jesus, life became simpler in so many ways. I've learned He wants me to come to Him first thing in the morning—get on my knees and pray for His grace for that day—ask Him to come into my life—help me love my husband and children—and yield my life to Him.

I started preparing for my Sundays on Saturday night. On Sundays, rather than racing and yelling, I started the day with prayer. Just entering into the day calmly works miracles in itself, of course!

I wondered if Bob and the children would see a difference. At first nobody commented at all, but one morning on the way to church I told Bob, "I've really tried to make Sunday mornings better lately."

"I've noticed that. You've been very good these last few Sundays," he said.

Then I knew it was working. Things were getting much smoother. As weeks rolled into months I began seeing this messy problem as an example of the sort of thing you think never can be overcome. It seems really tough at first—even impossible—but once habits are established it's like nothing. I still have mornings when I don't make it, when I fuss or complain, but problems no longer are the rule.

Saturday nights at the prayer altar I often pray, "Lord, You know I'm going to be cantankerous. I'll be tired and not want to get up tomorrow morning. Please help me get up and give me that grace, patience, love, and tolerance I need."

Bob and the children realize I know my failures and pray about them, and that seems to put a different light on things. Even children observe this sort of growth and respond to it. They cooperate. They see Sundays are nicer—with more understanding and sweetness on my part—and they know Jesus gets the credit.

Bob is much more emotionally mature than I, and while he's also older chronologically, I'm older in the Christian life. I did push him to form the habit of going to church and I admit I nagged him about it. Bob graciously says, however, that without my example he never would have seen the need for church and would not have gone.

To me, little victories lots of times seem bigger than so-called big victories. It's a thrill to overcome the early morning blues. I'm grateful to get up on Sundays with a happy heart, with more patience and love, and not pick on the faults of my spouse.

It helps to remember the words of the 118th Psalm:

THIS IS THE DAY WHICH THE LORD HAS MADE; WE WILL REJOICE AND BE GLAD IN IT.

Amen!

# 6

# God Gave Me These Babies

"Look, why don't you give in again?" Bob asked in a hard voice. His resentment stuck out a mile.

We disagreed about caring for Billy and Barbara, our three year olds.

Mary Hendrick, who had nursed them from the very beginning, had been offered an excellent new job—more money, fewer days. We could match that, of course, but money and hours weren't the issue. The problem was—and I knew the Lord allowed this to come up for a purpose—should we keep Mary? Or should I care for the twins myself?

I felt it was essential to keep Mary. After all, I looked after the twins a lot of the time; they certainly didn't lack their mother's attention. Other times, I wanted them to have the best substitute mother available.

Bob thought we had outgrown the need for a nursemaid. He wanted me to do it all—which seemed downright unfair, if not impossible. The more we talked, the less we solved. This became one of the rare times my husband and I truly disagreed about how to rear our children.

That night I came downstairs, apart from my family, to pray about the situation. God put a heavy burden on my heart. But I felt so angry, so full of self-pity, that at first I couldn't pray.

I was mad at Bob. And the more I reviewed my grievances, the madder I got. For some time, he'd been unsympathetic to what he considered my lack of involvement with our twins. I recalled a recent Sunday morning when Mary went to church with us. Bob, who likes Mary, said we should have gone to church just as a family. I felt upset that he disliked taking Mary with us—after all, I had led her to the Lord, and I care about her—so instead of listening to what Bob *really* was saying, I chose to misunderstand him.

"Every other mother in the country manages to take her kids to church without a nurse," Bob said. That was a real put-down. It hurt.

I really cried as I remembered that episode. When he said, "Every other mother does it," that cut me to the core. I *know* every other mother does it, but not every other mother is cobreadwinner, either.

I thought of Bob, upstairs in bed. He knew I was fighting it out down here. And when I thought how he'd said, "Look. Give in again if you want to," I almost hated him. He wasn't very understanding.

So I cried a while, and prayed a while. Then I reached for a bulletin someone sends me from Connecticut—a small publication called "A Woman's Epistle." For some reason I began to browse through it—and I found an article about a mother's responsibilities to her children. I read this as thoughtfully as if it were something I'd never before considered.

Mothers today need to take their responsibilities more seriously than ever, it said. Children are blessings from God, and it's important to be with them and oversee them every minute: teaching, training, bringing them up in the admonition of the Lord.

The article said nothing new to me. Nevertheless, it pierced my heart. I took a long, hard look at my "mothering" and had to admit it was too easy to turn the twins over to Mary every time the schedule got tough. I'd tell Mary to have them dressed by a certain time, and they'd be ready. I never seemed to be with them at rush hours. In all honesty, I knew they needed more discipline in certain areas of their little lives, too.

For a long time, I thought about these little ones. In my mind's eye I watched them every moment of a typical day, critically inspected my performance as their mother.

Did I need to give more of myself to these children? Should they be included more with the rest of the family? Did Billy and Barbara *want* to spend more time with Daddy and Mommy, Bobby, and Gloria?

I felt very sober now, as I began to pray. "Please, Lord, help me know Your will."

That morning, Brother Bill had preached about the Lord's Prayer. I thought about something he said, and reached for Grandma Berry's old Bible, the one Grandpa gave her in 1940, the year I was born. I turned to the front of the Bible, where Grandma had written out the Lord's Prayer and the Twenty-Third Psalm, in her old-fashioned handwriting.

It was like I'd never seen them before. The Lord's Prayer looked brand new. And when I read the Twenty-Third

Psalm, it hit me with real impact: The Lord is *my* shepherd. It's like I'm the only sheep He has.

If He is my personal shepherd, there's *nothing* I should want!

"Lord, You gave me these babies, then spared their lives, and You spared my life," I told Him. "Now You want me to go through the rough business of taking care of them. I took care of the first two, but then I was younger, Lord, and life was simpler.

"Is it that You want me to tackle the rough times again with *these* babies? Is there some reason I should?

"Because Lord, I just don't know how I'm going to do it. I don't see how I can maintain the schedule, run the household with all its problems, keep myself physically fit, attend to all the children, keep my husband happy, *and* meet our business obligations."

I felt so overwhelmed I began to cry harder than ever. Even as I wept, however, I saw how much I needed to confront myself with this situation. And did He show me! We had let Mary become the easy way out, I saw. She was becoming nervous with the children. Three-year-old twins are hard on anybody but especially a conscientious woman like Mary.

Still, she had them well trained and on schedule. The twins loved her. And when I thought of doing without Mary—all the things which could go wrong—I felt devastated.

"Lord, You know it's an impossible task for me or any other human being," I told Him at last. "I just can't do it all."

Silence. No answer. I knew that was a lie, because I had cared for the twins alone those first days at home, before their nurse arrived, and while it was hectic, I *did* manage.

They were so tiny and frail, and had to be fed every three hours—it was terrible.

How good of God to let me see I *could* take care of my twins those first days, I thought. I did it then, when they were so needy, so helpless. But surely He doesn't expect me to return to all that now, with life so complicated in this household?

But suddenly, with great clarity, I saw He did. God showed me our family situation had been getting out of hand. I saw He expected me to move completely into my area of responsibility. This upset me completely.

What would happen on Sundays? If I'd had trouble before, it would be chaos now! And what would I have to give up? Our Bible classes? Tennis lessons? What else?

Even as I resisted, I had to marvel once again at God's perfect timing—Mary's need, the twins' needs, Bob's feelings, our family as a whole—everything came together simultaneously. I bowed my head. "Dear Lord, You have brought me to this point. I know You are *my* shepherd, and I shall not want. I also know I can do *all* things through Christ, which strengtheneth me. Help me to obey Your will and realize, hour by hour, that Your grace is sufficient."

The sky was turning light when I trudged upstairs at last. I had struggled, pondered and prayed nearly all night. I looked down at Bob. Had I really been so angry with him, so filled with malice, only a few hours ago? I know Bob will help me, I thought.

Bob has probably the greatest patience with his children of any man I know. He's fantastic. Sometimes he's much more patient than I.

But also I know child care is primarily the woman's role. I can't rely on Bob or anyone else. It's my job.

In the morning, when I prayed, I thanked God for my decision. I felt really good about it—relieved to the point I almost felt lighthearted. Therefore I felt surprised, when I told Bob, to see him turn white as a sheet.

"Are you sure?", he asked, sounding shocked. Then he said, "Okay, Anita, if that's what you want."

"Will you back me up, Bob? Will you help me?"

"Of course." But I knew he didn't yet realize how big my decision was.

Mary was surprised too. She wanted to stay—if I needed her. But she accepted my decision, knowing I had prayed about it, and I could see she saw it was for the best. It was best for her, for me, and for the babies. Mary is a hard worker, has a heart good as gold, and loved my babies like they were her own flesh and blood.

The first few nights were really tough, but I was determined not to complain. I'd made my own decision, had accepted a challenge. Then too, there's that stubborn streak in me that wants to find out.

"I really can't do it," the weak part of me would whisper a dozen times a day. I'd think of all the problems weighing on me, and want to go under. Then the part of me that's of the Lord would say, "Just step out on faith. He'll do it. You won't have to do anything alone."

Naturally we prayed about these things at the family altar. Bob particularly was really sweet. He asked God to help Mommy so I wouldn't get too tired, and that during this adjustment, everyone would work together.

Then came Sunday morning—the real test. I had been sleeping downstairs in the nursery, apart from Bob and the older kids, and I didn't really rest too well. That first Sunday morning I got up at 5:30, dog-tired but determined to get a good start.

Bob pitched in and cooked breakfast. He told the kids to be extra good because Mommy needed help. The children, even the babies, really responded. Bobby and Gloria were unusually efficient that morning. Usually they're slow, and Gloria interrupts me as I try to dress: "Pull up my zipper, Mommy. Please fix my hair."

However, that day Gloria helped me dress Barbara and Billy. Bobby and Bob cleared away the breakfast dishes. And everything went smoothly—until the station wagon wouldn't start. The whole family had prayed for grace, so we stayed amazingly calm. We all piled in the other car and got to Sunday school only a few minutes late. And there wasn't the usual turmoil—cantankerous kids, flustered mommy, mad daddy.

Things didn't always go so well, though. I stayed sleepy and cranky and would get very cross—even cry—by afternoon some days. I learned to pray about it, asking for grace and peace, and for the Lord to calm my nerves. I turned to a complete reliance on the Lord.

God doesn't expect us to sit on our hands. I saw He intended me to exert real physical and mental effort. It represented a big step of faith on my part—maybe one of my biggest—because my new efforts dug into some time and energy previously reserved for business. I tried not to think about that too much; I had resolved to take things day by day.

To everybody's surprise, we started having a new kind of fun as a family. We'd had togetherness in our prayer life, but this was a different kind of closeness. We began to see we had given away a lot of privacy in the past. Also, as we began to pull the twins into all our family doings we saw they *belonged* there. They seemed to mature almost over-night.

Bob really did help me. Sometimes he took over in the kitchen, and I was astonished to discover I married a talented cook. One night he cooked a perfect hungarian goulash, and another time two quiche lorraines. Gloria helped her daddy in the kitchen, and we dined by candlelight.

But it was Bobby who came up with the best idea of all. I had been sleeping downstairs with the twins, and I hated the isolation. (The babies must have hated it all this time too, I had to admit to myself.) As we discussed the problem of our family's being separated into two distinct areas of our big house, Bobby had an inspiration.

"Mommy, why don't you let Billy sleep with me? He can use the trundle bed under my bed."

"Bobby, you know that would never work!"

Then I reconsidered. His idea simply was too tempting to resist.

"Still, if we got a trundle bed for Gloria and put Barbara in with her, I could return to the master bedroom. We'd all be upstairs together!"

Despite the plan's trouble potential, we ordered another trundle bed immediately. I had no idea how the roommate system would work, but it seemed worth a try.

The first night produced unexpected results. Mary often had trouble getting the twins to sleep; sometimes they'd entertain one another until ten o'clock. But Bobby and Gloria didn't let them talk and play, so by eight o'clock that night all four kids were sound asleep. The twins knew they had to be good so they'd get to sleep there again.

Bobby and Gloria astonished us as they took over with the twins in ways we didn't dream they could. One morning,

# From our family album

**(Bob took most of these pictures, which is why he isn't in many!)**

Christmas at our house: We love our live twelve-foot tree with ornaments from Sweden and other countries in the world. Tree trimming is a family project. *Below:* Christmas is a family time and Bob and I feel fortunate to have ours with us at Villa Verde on Jesus' birthday. On the left-hand side of the dining-room table are Farmor (Bob's mother), Gloria, Farfar (Bob's father), and Billy. On the other side are my mother, Bobby, Daddy George (my step-father), and Barbara.

Bob took this picture at the heart of our home — our family altar. We were all thrilled when he surprised us with the altar but we had no idea what it would mean to us as a family.

Highlight of Easter was a visit from Billy Graham and Grady Wilson on Good Friday. Here he is with Peggy and Bill Chapman (Brother Bill is our pastor) and Charlie Morgan. (That's Billy in the subdued shirt!) *Below:* Dinnertime outside in the gallery: On the left, Jody and Bobby wait for Gloria and I to serve them, while on the right—equally patient —are Grady Wilson, Billy Graham, and Barbara.

We love this picture of Barbara with her Easter basket. *Below:*
All dressed up and a special place to go — church! Bob took this
picture of us in the courtyard on Easter morning.

Here are two of my sisters-in-Christ: Charlotte Topping and Marabel Morgan. *Below*: This picture was taken at Disney World where we combined business and pleasure making commercials for the Florida Citrus Commission.

And here's our Kathie — Kathie Epstein. We first met her at the Junior Miss Pageant where she represented her home state of Maryland. She went to Israel when we did and baby-sat for us. Now she is very much a part of our home as my personal secretary and very dear friend, as well as a capable pinch hitter for me all over the country. (Photo by Philip Yancey of *Campus Life*)

Bob blows out the candle on his birthday cake at a great Italian restaurant in Israel. Since Bob's of Swedish descent, it was quite an international occasion!

With the Mount of Olives serving as a background, here are Bob and I with Bobby and Gloria Lynn. The older children accompanied us on this never-to-be-forgotten trip to the Holy Land.

This was taken at Northwest Baptist Church Vacation Bible School during a popcorn break while I was a teacher at the school. That's Brother Charlie Walker feeding me on the left, and Brother Bill Chapman laughing on the right. *Below:* Thanksgiving Day. What a lot we have to be thankful for! This was a family reunion for us. In the front row are my niece Lisa Page (age 8), then Gloria and Bobby, then Michele Page (age 6), and my mother Lenore Cate holding Barbara with Kathy Page (age 13), standing next to Mother. In the back row are Bob, Billy, and me, then Daddy George Cate, Grandpa Berry, my sister Sandra Page, and her husband Sam.

as I began to dress the twins to take them downstairs with me, Billy balked.

"No, Mommy. I want to go downstairs with Bobby."

"I'll take care of him, Mommy," Bobby offered.

As I hesitated, Gloria spoke up. "We'll take care of the babies, Mommy. You go fix breakfast. Don't worry. We *know* *how* to take care of them!"

I did worry, but then I saw I needed to give the older kids that responsibility. It has worked out great. We're amazed at how much Bobby and Gloria teach the little ones.

Billy almost worships his big brother. He follows Bobby around like a little shadow. Gloria and Barbara encountered some friction, however; they're both headstrong and competitive. Still, Barbara is the kid who really has shaped up. She had developed a habit of crying when things didn't go to suit her. She had to learn to cooperate.

The whole venture seemed shaky some of those first days, however. The advantages seemed offset by my fatigue and crankiness, and I knew my kids didn't get the best side of me. I was yelling at them and spanking them. "Lord, is this good?" I'd ask. I questioned whether I had taken on too much.

The girls in my Sunday school class helped resolve that. I crept in that first morning with circles under my eyes and told what was happening. I was physically tired and mentally despondent by then—a pretty meek character. They all prayed for me.

When Bobby and Gloria proved so capable with the twins, it seemed those prayers were answered. But as the older children shared their rooms with the little ones, naturally some battles occurred. We told the twins Gloria's doll house and Bobby's train set were off limits. Bobby and Gloria had to learn some give-and-take, and the twins got spanked, too, for breaking the rules about toys.

Eventually the newness wore off, and when the twins no longer were a novelty, Bobby and Gloria were ready to send them back downstairs.

"No. Nothing doing," Bob said decisively. "We are a family again, and we all share the responsibility. Besides, Bobby and Gloria, we need your help."

"Okay, Daddy," our older children said, looking proud. From then on they certainly did their share. For our part, Bob and I saw that Bobby and Gloria needed that responsibility.

One postscript to the story concerns this book. The publisher's agreement had been on my desk for weeks. Bob had been after me to sign it, as had Dick Shack, my agent, who helped persuade me to do the first two books, but I just didn't sign.

One day soon after Mary left, as I thought about all the ways God was changing us as a Christian family, I knew He wanted me to start the book. I had not felt certain before, but now it came through clear as a bell. I picked up the phone.

"Bob, please call the publishers and say we'll do the book."

"Okay, Anita," Bob said, not sounding particularly surprised.

It was as though God were telling me, "Do it now while you're going through these difficulties, while everything is still fresh." I realized we had not been a complete family before then. Although things had seemed smooth, they were not as God would have them be.

Of course He didn't let our situation develop for the sake of a book! But in His perfect plan He wants to use the lessons we are learning—and will learn—in constructive ways. God doesn't bring us to the hard place, but when we put ourselves there, He can redeem any situation in all sorts of creative ways.

Earlier I had thought there was absolutely no time to write another book. The schedule was too tight. But now when it's *incredibly* tight—here goes!

When I phoned Charlotte Topping and Marabel Morgan to tell them I'd decided to do the book, they were shocked.

"How in the world will you do it?" Charlotte asked.

"You know how I'm going to do it."

"Well, Anita, you'll have my prayers."

"I know," I told her, laughing a little. "What in the world do you think I called you for?"

And the girls in my Sunday school class! I'd dragged in so wilted and tired one week, begging for their prayers. The very next Sunday I told them that because of all that was happening, I had decided to begin a new book. They rejoiced with my decision and promised to pray for the book. How great to have all those prayers, giving added support!

And now I'll share the most beautiful part of all—just to show you how God, when you take a step for Him, immediately will bless your heart.

I began taking care of the twins on a Friday. The following day a specialist from the Mailman Center for Child Development through the University of Miami clinic which specializes in brain damage cases was scheduled to evaluate our twins. We had set up the appointment weeks earlier.

Doctors all along had stressed the possibility of some brain damage due to the difficulties surrounding these babies' births. Since I had been in shock for two hours before Barbara was born, our pediatrician felt particular concern for her.

Any damage the twins sustained could best be determined between ages two and five. Our pediatrician warned us to expect some impairment. Barbara does have a small physical problem, a slightly awkward walk, which the specialist says she'll outgrow. He describes it as "a small chip in a perfect dish."

The specialist came to our house and examined each child separately, administering several tests. As he worked with Billy alone, you can imagine my feelings of apprehension.

"Whatever happens, it really doesn't matter," I told myself. "We gave these children to the Lord. We're ready to accept His will for them." I almost didn't care to know the diagnosis —except, of course, we needed to know if there were any hindrance to the learning process.

As he tested Barbara, I really did feel somewhat nervous. A parent always thinks his children are bright. Still, I recalled how doctors from the outset had urged us to test the babies. "They must think something's wrong," I told myself.

At last the doctor came in and sat with us. He just looked at us for a moment, and shook his head.

"First, there's no sign of any brain damage whatsoever," he said, sounding perplexed. "That's rather miraculous. I have tested many children with backgrounds similar to yours —premature births, similar physical histories. I can't tell you how lucky you are.

"Not only are they normal, with no sign of brain damage, but your children have superior intelligence."

"You're kidding!" I blurted out. I felt almost too amazed to absorb the news.

"No, I'm not kidding," he said, smiling. "They're really well above average. You have no idea what lucky, lucky people you are."

"Sir, luck has nothing to do with it," I told him firmly. "The babies almost died, and I almost died in childbirth. I guess you know the story."

"Yes."

"They were prayed for. They are the results of those prayers. We all are. When God does something, He does it right. Only He should get the glory for this—but we get the blessings of it."

He grinned at me, looking fully as delighted as I felt. "You're probably right. I have no other explanation for it. I came expecting the worst. Very rarely do I have the privilege of giving good news. I'm so pleased about it. *Somebody* up there must like you!"

You can imagine our gratitude to God. The next day my heart overflowed as I shared this story with my Sunday school class. Those girls had prayed for us, had stayed so close to our family when we were in desperate need.

Now, many months later, we marveled together at what the Lord had done. They were overjoyed for Bob and me.

# 7

*Bob Green*

# A Man's Faith

I never dreamed I'd become the kind of guy who prays about things. Even five years ago the idea of praying before signing a contract, hiring a secretary, or placing a phone call would have seemed 'way out to me.

Realistically, I never expected to go that far with my Christian beliefs. Some men get saved on Tuesday and by Wednesday they're reading the Bible, teaching and all the rest of it. But I'm just not that kind of guy.

Of course, I'd had to start practically from scratch. I had attended Sunday school as a kid, but by the time I went to college, served in the air force and had a few years in radio, all that seemed pretty remote.

Then you fall in love with a Christian girl—and her commitment to Christ is very real. Anita's Christian faith was something I truly respected. However, I can't say I wanted it for myself—not at first.

Ignorant as I was then about life in Christ, I nevertheless recognized this love for Him as part of what made Anita the kind of girl I wanted. I knew she would be a good wife and mother.

The night before our wedding Gloria Roe, our close friend and sister in Christ, as well as one of America's top pianists and composers of sacred songs, helped lead me to the Lord. That was twelve years ago. It was a sincere commitment on my part, but I had little idea—really—of what it would mean.

At first, it meant that when Anita and I would have a bad fight we'd get on our knees and pray together. Then we'd make up. We didn't pray together on a regular basis—I couldn't imagine something like that! or even very often. Only in extreme need.

It also meant I became willing to go to church with her. When we first walked into Northwest Baptist they were meeting in a big quonset hut. They hadn't built their main sanctuary at that time. But the first and lasting impression that hit us was, the vast majority of the people there had their Bibles with them—and *open*.

To us, going to church without a Bible is like a student going to school without a book. It just doesn't make sense to go to church if you don't carry your Bible. If you don't feel the need to carry one, the preacher up there is not preaching from the Bible. In order to put the most he can into his sermon he's going to have to refer to the Bible, and you are going to have to use it.

If a couple is looking for a church home and they go to a church where they see a lot of Bibles and hear a lot of pages turn, they can be sure the preacher is teaching the Word. In the cases where he is not teaching the Word, it may not be his fault. But in that case, he's not head of his church as he should be.

The most important thing after a person is saved is fellowship with like-believers. After a man is saved he's like a newborn baby. He needs that nourishing fellowship, or he'll starve to death and fall by the wayside.

Fortunately, Anita insisted that we go to church. She couldn't live without it. I knew this and went along with her gladly—though for a long time I felt she wanted to go too often. We didn't hassle too much about it, though. She insisted, and mostly I went along.

Then came our children, and I wanted Bobby and Gloria to have the kind of early Christian training Anita had. I wanted it to start early and consistently, and become a natural part of their lives. By the time the twins arrived, seeing the faith Bobby and Gloria already had by ages five and six, I was convinced this training should start in the crib.

No problem—except for one thing. The very nature of a Christian upbringing, as outlined in the Bible, requires two parents—a mother and a father. The man is considered to be the priest to his household. To turn these responsibilities over to his wife is, in the sight of God, a complete cop-out.

Well, like too many other men, I can't claim I was the spiritual head of our household. It wasn't possible for me to jump into Christianity that way. Anita's thing last year was that I had to develop as a leader. I said, "Look, everybody has to develop at their own pace. Nobody knows what's in somebody else's heart."

Looking back, we both see the Lord has dealt with me in His own good time. And both of us—my wife as well as myself—stepped off into a whole new world of faith when the twins were born.

Our crisis with the twins (after their doctor told us they were dying) brought us to our knees with Brother Bill in Anita's hospital room. Brother Bill asked if we were willing to give those babies to God—*no matter what His will for them might be.* It took much prayer to bring us to that point. But when I realized I still would love God *no matter what He decided,* there was a peace I'd never known before. Neither of us had been that severely tested before; and until your faith is tested, you can't know if it will hold.

Anita nearly died. The twins nearly died. When a guy faces that kind of thing, something in his life has to give. I learned I literally cannot make it without Jesus Christ.

After that miracle happened in our lives—what with people's prayers, and the twins' lives spared—more than ever I felt the importance of Christian witnessing. I wanted people to know God. More than ever, therefore, I bugged Anita to witness. I still think being able to witness is one of the greatest gifts—one of the most marvelous blessings—a Christian can have.

I guess that's why I've always pushed Anita to witness. I knew she had Christ in her life. I wanted her to show Him to others.

For myself, I still wasn't ready. I longed to tell people about Jesus, but felt I was too unprepared. Anita accused me of making *her* do what I really wanted to do myself—and there's some truth to that. Still, God has to bring me to exactly the right place before I can give my testimony, and I know He will.

Actually, there's no way a Christian can justify *not* witnessing. In the service I trained thousands of men, yet in all those years, despite all the men I had contact with, not one ever told me about Jesus. Not one boy ever came to me and witnessed.

Suppose one had. What if I had become converted to Christ? As a Christian, a sergeant who instructed thousands of trainees, maybe I would have witnessed to those thousands. I think of the wasted years!

Several years ago, visiting the home of Senator and Mrs. Mark Hatfield, we were impressed to see they had a family prayer altar. "Isn't that great!" Anita and I both said. We'd never seen one in a home before. I mentioned to Mark Hatfield that I'd sure love to know about it if he ever saw another antique altar like theirs. Meanwhile, everywhere I went, I looked for an altar. Eventually Mark Hatfield did find one, and had it shipped to me. I had it restored, then slipped it upstairs into our bedroom to surprise Anita.

I knew she wanted it, and I liked the idea too. But neither of us dreamed how much this one thing would open up our family life. We already had established pretty good prayer habits, I guess, but the altar strengthened things even more.

Here's a quiet place—set apart from all hustle-bustle—where anyone can go when he has a problem. The kids often slip in to the altar to pray alone. Also, it's the place we congregate at the end of each day, to pray as a family.

Here, when we pray to God, others in the family hear also—and pray with us. The kids' prayers are very illuminating. Often you're really surprised at how mature and unselfish they are. And sometimes they're amusing—like when Bobby and Gloria pray the twins will learn not to fidget so much at the altar!

The twins often come up with good prayers. Billy prays the monster won't get him, that he won't be afraid of thunder and lightning, and, "I pray that Jesus will help me stop sucking my thumb."

He still sucks his thumb, but he's praying about it.

Barbara had a thing about her rubber nipple pacifier. She

was really attached to it. She prayed that Jesus would help her not use it any more. One Sunday she went out and stood on the dock and threw that nipple into Biscayne Bay—and that's the last we ever heard of it from her.

We were so tickled. It was her own voluntary act, and it shows you even a two-and-one-half-year-old baby can have a faith that witnesses to a grown man.

The rest of us threw a spontaneous little party for Barbara. We put a candle on a cupcake, and made a big thing of it. Billy brags on his twin for throwing her nipple in the bay, and he keeps praying he'll learn to stop sucking his thumb. The twins have very practical prayers.

The kids' requests reveal what kind of people they are. For example, Bobby often prays about his homework—that he'll apply himself better and do better work. Gloria often prays for her friends who don't know Jesus, and for the parents who don't know Jesus.

The point is, our children don't just kneel down and go through sing-song stuff. They really talk to Jesus. I wish I had known Him that way at their age.

Through our daily prayer life, everybody in my family witnesses to me continually. Like Anita's Sunday morning problems; she didn't talk to me about that, she prayed about it. And the Lord gave her self-control. Anita prayed, and she worked. And I immediately noticed a difference.

As soon as people (like me!) get angry and are about to give a nasty retort—if they can pray for about five seconds— that will take the edge off immediately. Then they should try to hold off on their reaction.

"Boy, I'm really mad, and really concerned, and I'm really going to blow up," they should say. "If it's really important to blow up over this, I'm going to get very angry a half-hour from now." Then forget it for half an hour. If it's still important enough to get mad about then, get mad! Surprising how often that first little prayer takes care of the whole thing, though.

Little prayers and big prayers. Who knows which is which? Only God. And the night Anita went downstairs to wrestle with herself, to pray about the twins. Who else may have been praying for her—besides me—that night? We'll never know.

We do know God hears your requests. Anita made the right decision. To really know your children, you've got to see them through good things and difficult things. We might have been getting into a groove where you let somebody else take care of your children—let them do the dirty stuff while you miss the screaming and aggravating and all those things which are really important to be a part of.

We've seen a significant difference in the twins. They're much more content. We're more tired, but they're happier. They're a real part of the family now, and Bobby and Gloria are much more of an influence on them than they were before. They've taught the twins a lot.

Even without an altar, families can set aside a special place in their home where it's practical to assemble for prayer. In a den, in front of the living room sofa, any place will do so long as everyone congregates there.

I don't believe there are many families who pray together. I don't mean "now I lay me down to sleep," but sincere cries for help. Knowing their children are in there every night praying for real problems—praying about sickness and school work, for Mommy and Daddy's needs. Imagine the benefits of a whole family's knowing what's on one another's mind, what sins each one is struggling with. Imagine hearing parents and children together, confessing, praising, and giving thanks!

I'd urge any man to build an altar for his home—or order

one from a church supply house. Or, lacking space for one, start assembling your family for prayer each day, even if it's around the dining table or seated on the floor. This one habit could completely transform your family. We know.

Talk about witnessing, prayer, church-going, and you have to assess exactly where God's Word places in your life. Because unless you read your Bible faithfully and regularly, you'll never be able to make it in these other areas.

In 1 Peter 2:2 the Apostle Paul said, "As newborn babes, desire the sincere milk of the word, that ye may grow thereby."

Second Timothy 3:16, 17 says:

All scripture is given by inspiration of God, and is profitable for doctrine, for reproof, for correction, for instruction in righteousness; That the man of God may be perfect, thoroughly furnished unto all good works.

That says it. And that's why I believe the husband who intends to head his household, assuming full responsibility for it, must read his Bible daily. He needs all the inspiration and instruction he can get!

Another thing, the Bible is a fascinating set of books. Get started reading these on any kind of regular basis, and I guarantee you'll find it hard to quit. Bobby and Gloria take turns reading portions of Scripture at breakfast, which starts everybody's day well at our house. Anita and I and the two older children also have private Bible reading and study, and we refer often to our Bibles during the course of a day.

Back in America's good old days, when parents were more authoritative and children less discontent, fathers used God as their authority. Where parents and children read the

Bible, it's not so much "do this because I say to," but "do this because God says so, and you love Him." Thus parental discipline and training becomes what it's meant to be—a loving extension of God's rules for life.

Sometimes when Anita and I travel to other parts of the country we visit churches where you never hear the name Jesus mentioned in an entire sermon, nor any mention made of God's Word. We must get back to the Bible. People don't want to go to church to hear about "the man upstairs." They want to know about Jesus who died on the cross for us. They want the real thing.

When they asked Charlie Morgan and me to share a twelfth-grade-Sunday-school class a few months back, we had to dig in to the Bible. We have a class of twenty-seven, and are trying to hang on to them for the Lord. They're at an age when so many kids drop out of church.

Charlie and I agreed that getting them interested in the Word is the foundation. The more you read it, the more you want to learn. And when you begin to witness, you really have to know your subject matter. People can really ask some questions. You can't rely on your own knowledge or reasoning, but only on what the Word says.

If you cite the Bible as your standard, whether or not they respect what *you* say, they must accept the Bible as your authority. Once you establish that, there's little they can argue with.

You can't say, "Look, I'm Bob Green and I believe you must do so-and-so . . . ."

They can shoot you down in flames. But if you quote from the Bible, they can't argue with you. They believe it's the Word, or they don't.

I think you should take advantage of any opportunity you get to discuss Jesus. The devil makes many other opportunities available for talking against the Lord. Popular magazines, television, and all kinds of other things constantly work against us. Christians need to stand up for Jesus.

Nowadays in a mixed group anything goes—conversationally. Few topics make a woman blush. Nothing bothers them anymore because they have seen everything. Mutter any four-letter word in conversation with a lot of people and it wouldn't faze them a bit. They've seen it in print, in motion pictures, and on television.

But mention the word "Jesus"—and watch people grow ill at ease. It's amazing how flustered sophisticates sometimes get at any reference to Jesus Christ.

A man—particularly a family man—needs to figure out what his life stands for. The Bible describes what God wants a man to be, in every respect—to his wife, children, work, neighbors, his faith, and everything else important. Also, the Bible speaks to men about success.

If you must seek success, try for spiritual success. Forget about bigger houses, more cars, and that sort of thing. That's not real wealth. How much are you filled with the Lord? That's a better measure of wealth.

Anita and I attend a very wealthy church, but few of its members have big incomes. They are rich in the Lord. You see their standard of living—a *spiritual* standard—and you want it for yourself.

*8*

# Friends and Brothers

Bob and I yearned for Christian friends.

A year ago—still fairly new to our neighborhood—we felt almost totally alone. We had such hunger for fellowship with like-believers, and there seemed a real lack of it here.

But God knows our needs before we ask Him. Today there are at least half a dozen fellow prayer-group members in our area. In fact, some attend as a result of my witnessing to them.

We never actually prayed for these special new friendships, but God sent them to us anyhow. When He gave me the burden of witnessing, He knew in His fantastic wisdom that this also would bring about the fellowship our family so needed. Gradually a Christian community is growing around us.

We need that community. Your family also needs the love and fellowship which can enter a Christian home from those in the world outside. The Bible says in Proverbs 17:17, "A friend loveth at all times, and a brother is born for adversity." We need all the friends and brothers we can get!

If your family is church-centered, Christian friends should very easily appear in your lives. Church becomes an important source of meaningful friendships. The Word tells us to confess our faults one to the other (James 5:16), and our problems. That's why we need a church where the Spirit of God leads you—where there's love and fellowship and personal prayer.

My Sunday school class, for example, involves every gal in it. We ask for prayers. As I've shared with you earlier, you can walk into that room with your chin dragging the floor, and every other woman offers comfort. When you have joy, all rejoice with you. When some small trial comes into my life, I phone several of the girls in the class—and they pray for me.

In other words, this kind of fellowship is real, constant, and something you can count on—because it is of God. Families lacking this type relationship are missing something vitally important. Not only do you need the sort of Christian friends who rally in times of crisis, but also you need to know they need *your* love, *your* prayers, too. All of us need to be needed.

Very intimate friendships grow out of prayer groups. As the Holy Spirit added girls to our group, it grew into a very precious unit. Some came through Marabel Morgan's witness during her "Total Woman" course. These girls, with some friends I had led to Christ, began to meet regularly for prayer, sharing and Bible study. By witnessing to these souls we've created a group of born-again believers, which has given us the fellowship we need.

This extends to our children because it sets an example

of how new friends are added on by the Lord—how we strengthen friendships, pray for friends, and care for one another.

Bob really needed Christian male companionship. Men need purely male interests and activities, just as we gals like our hen-party-type affairs. Some wives make the big mistake of trying to preempt all their husband's time, feeling jealous of hours he spends with the "boys" on fishing trips and the like.

The Bible speaks of Christian brothers, and this truly can be something beautiful. When Bob went forward at our church last year to become a fisherman for the Lord (which means he pledges to witness daily for Christ), Charlie Morgan followed him to the altar.

Charlie and Bob love one another in the Lord. Bob never before had a chance for such close friendship, especially with a fellow believer. Today he and Charlie are like brothers. I really praise the Lord for it.

As their friendship first developed, however, I admit Marabel and I sometimes got rather turned off. Our men were on the phone with one another constantly, always going somewhere together, talking, planning, sharing, until Marabel and I felt almost neglected.

Well, time took care of that. Everything smoothed out, of course, with the result that Bob and Charlie became brothers in the Lord, and Marabel and I, sisters.

Marabel and Charlie are such an important part of our lives in every way—social, witnessing, sharing, and praying. Whenever I'm about to witness to someone, I ask Marabel to pray for me. Before each of her "Total Woman" classes begins, I stop for a moment and pray for that.

Proverbs 18:24 describes the art of friendship in a lovely

way: "A man that hath friends must shew himself friendly: and there is a friend that sticketh closer than a brother."

That's Marabel. She has become one of my dearest friends. I can show her my real self—my ugly self—knowing she'll not judge or reject me. Gloria Roe and I always were like that but we see one another too seldom these days, since Gloria lives in California. Marabel and I are like two peas in a tight pod. We share one another's problems.

Last fall I had a recording date in Nashville. Bob's father had surgery at that time so Bob couldn't go with me. Marabel accompanied me instead. First we flew to Chicago for a convention, then on to Nashville for recording. We had a ball.

This was so refreshing for me. Only once or twice a year am I able to have a lunch date with the gals, and I miss that kind of stuff. Just to be with a friend, to share and laugh and be silly—oh, it was great!

Marabel overwhelms me because she's so consistent in her nature. There's no way you'll see her frown, or get cross or angry. She may get cool if she's distressed, but still it's in a gentle, loving kind of way. She has a glow about her. Everybody who knows Marabel sees Jesus in her, just like a shining light.

"You make me sick," I tell her sometimes, kidding, "going around with that happy smile on your face, saying, 'God has a wonderful plan for your life!' "

She believes it, too.

I love Marabel. She is so much the opposite of me. She's more like the Apostle Paul, while I'm like Peter—walking on the water, then sinking! We both want to be disciples of Christ, but there's a tremendous difference in the two of us. I can consistently go to her and get strength for my spiritual life. We truly are Christian sisters.

I didn't realize I had a need for Marabel. That's a relationship I didn't ask for, but God gave it to me just the same. I had prayed for Bob to receive a Christian friend, and I recall asking for fellowship, but I don't remember asking for a friend for myself. Yet that need has been met also.

With friendship or anything else, God knows our needs long before we ask Him. He wants to hear us ask Him—to make ourselves available to Him—and for us to yield ourselves daily. He expects us to tell Him our needs, talk to Him, and be honest. Jesus says, "If ye abide in me and my words abide in you, ye shall ask what ye will and it shall be done unto you" (John 15:7).

He didn't promise to fill every heart's desire but He did instruct us to ask. Therefore, if you need brothers and sisters in the Lord, ask. God knows. He'll fill the needs He sees, and He sees perfectly. Hebrews 13:1, 2, a beautiful passage, advises:

> Let brotherly love continue.
> Be not forgetful to entertain strangers: for thereby some have entertained angels unawares.

When we first met some of the Miami Dolphins football players, it was like discovering "angels" in a way I wouldn't have thought of. Bob and Charlie, naturally, were the ones interested in football. Marabel and I merely showed a polite interest because of our husbands—and then we got to know some of the Christian players, and their wives.

Bob Griese and his wife Judy, Howard Twilley and Julie, Mike and Nancy Kolen, Norm and Bobbie Evans, Tim and Connie Foley, Bob and Carol Heinz, Bob and Bonnie Kuechenberg, Karl and Stephanie Noonan, John and Stacy Richardson—what outstanding couples to count as friends!

Norm Evans and his wife are two of our favorites. Norm

has written a book titled *On God's Squad*. He gave a moving testimony at our church. It hasn't been easy for Norm to maintain his testimony. Some of the fellows kid him, and call him "Pope Norm."

Many of the Dolphins' wives have taken Marabel Morgan's "Total Woman" course. Also, Judy Griese, Julie Twilley, Marabel and I sometimes play tennis doubles.

Sometimes at the prayer altar, special friends pop into your mind for no reason you can think of: Milt and Carol Oshins. Bob and Milt worked together in radio years ago, and the Oshins helped us make one of the most important decisions of our lives—to adopt a baby.

Then there were precious times when Vonda Van Dyke and I prayed together at our family altar. Vonda, a former Miss America, a talented performer and a beautiful girl, has written books you may have read. She lives in Miami, and Christ recently has led us to a deeper understanding of one another. Also do we hold in our Christian fellowship circle our dear friends George and Maureen Davis.

When Renny Berry, my cousin, moved here with his wife Janet last year, that was a blessing beyond anything I'd ever have prayed for. Renny, like his father, my Uncle Luther, is a Southern Baptist minister. His relationship to me is unique, because he has become as a brother to me—something new in my life. Renny is one of the very few men I've ever been able to share with, freely and honestly, in true Christian friendship. He holds a spot in my life comparable to that of Marabel, her Christian male counterpart. We take our problems to one another as brother and sister.

See how the Lord adds fascinating friends to our lives? He'll bring new friends and brothers to your life also, if you ask Him. Equally wonderful, He'll help you treasure friends from the past, and help those relationships grow.

Phil and Minna Braunstein, two special favorites in our family, have known Bob and me from the early days of our marriage. Phil is our financial advisor. I think of Phil and Minna in my hospital room three years ago, heads bowed, tears flowing down their cheeks, as a girl from my church prayed aloud for our desperately-ill twins.

My own tears were as much tears of gratitude for Phil, Minna, and our Northwest Baptist friends as for anything else. Though the Braunsteins are not Christians, they have come to church with Bob and me, on occasion.

Recently Phil said, "I can see you and Bob changing. You've outlived the rough spots in your marriage. You do try to live your faith." Some of our newer friends don't know Bob and I once had a rocky marriage. Phil and Minna have loved us through many difficulties, and we treasure them.

There's a lot of wisdom in that little verse the children sing:

> Make new friends, but keep the old;
> One is silver, the other is gold.

Phil and Minna Braunstein are purest gold.

As the Bible says, "Love is of God." He wants us, as Christians, to adopt new friends and cherish old ones, to allow Christ to make new relationships and maintain old ties. And it was Jesus who in John 15:12–14 said the greatest words any man ever spoke about friendship:

> This is my commandment, That ye love one another, as I have loved you.
> Greater love hath no man than this, that a man lay down his life for his friends.
> Ye are my friends, if ye do whatsoever I command you.

# 9

# *Journey to Jerusalem*

"Let's take Bobby and Gloria," Bob said.

"Are you *kidding?*"

"Look, Anita, things are very tense in the Middle East. It may be years before we can get back to Israel. Imagine what this trip could do for the kids; to walk where Jesus walked—see the places they're reading about in the Bible— make the whole thing come alive to them."

I just stared at Bob. Drag two young children halfway around the world? Ten days in Israel, traveling, sight-seeing, with no baby sitter?

We were to attend the Conference on Biblical Prophecy in Jerusalem. We had decided spontaneously, abruptly, and our excitement was building by the day. For me, the trip represented the fulfillment of a lifelong dream. I'd longed to go to Israel since I was a child. I knew nothing of the land in which Jesus lived and died, and knew all too little about the Bible.

Now Bob and I would make the pilgrimage together. I praised the Lord for what this could mean to our relationships, individual and shared, with Him. And how wonderful, we thought, if some of our Spirit-filled friends also could go along. Charles and Marabel Morgan arranged to go, and from California came word that Gloria Roe and her husband, Ron Robertson, would meet us there.

As we studied our Bibles, preparing for whatever God meant us to experience, my heart almost burst at thoughts of what we'd soon share.

Then Bob suggested taking the kids. It seemed too wildly impractical an idea even to consider, but Bob continued to argue for it. At last we decided to ask Bobby and Gloria how *they* felt about it—just to get a reaction. I didn't really expect much enthusiasm. To my surprise, however, both children were intensely eager.

"Neat!" Bobby yelled. "What I want to see, Daddy, is where Jesus said, 'I'll make you fishers of men.' "

After making it a matter of faith, Bob and I decided to take the kids. I didn't quite see how we'd attend the conference and do everything else we wanted to do, but we agreed to ask the Lord to provide. That decision was to have far-reaching consequences.

Within two weeks from the time we decided to take the children to Israel, the Lord supplied us with a baby sitter. Kathie Epstein came to us from a very unlikely source.

Bob and I were filling a booking at the Junior Miss Pageant in Mobile, Alabama, where Bob happened to chat with Kathie one day. Not only did Bob discover this pretty, intelligent junior miss from Maryland to be a born-again Christian, but he was astounded to discover her dad had given her a very special high school graduation present: Kathie, with her mother, was to attend the Conference on Biblical Prophecy!

I love the funny way Kathie tells what happened next. "When Bob learned Mom and I were going to Jerusalem, he went sorta crazy," she said. "He grabbed me by the hand and rushed me to Anita's room. We burst through the door with him yelling, 'Anita, Anita! Our prayers have been answered!'

"I wondered what in the world was happening to me. This was like nothing I ever expected—not in my superwildest dreams. How could I be an answer to their prayers? Then my bubble burst. Bob said, 'Here's the *baby sitter* we prayed for!' "

In Jerusalem, Kathie did take care of Bobby and Gloria several times. She proved ideal to our needs, a delightful "provision" from the Lord. Much as we enjoyed Kathie then, however, we didn't dream she'd reappear in our lives months later—and the Lord would supply new directions to Kathie, Bob, and myself.

For weeks before our trip, Bob and I had pored over our Bibles, preparing our hearts for what we might experience in Israel. We had little idea of what to expect. We could never have anticipated the lasting impact those ten days were to make on our lives.

As we searched God's Word, we began to gain some small idea of the enormous importance of that relatively small area of Holy Land we'd visit. We'd see places where Jesus walked and talked, and touched the lives of so many people; where His disciples followed Him and denied Him, where they fell asleep during His anguish in the garden of Gethsemane.

In Matthew 23:37, we read how Jesus once yearned over

Jerusalem, a city He loved, where He preached, taught and healed—and, eventually came to trial and was put to death.

And then we were there, with our friends, viewing the same teeming, crooked streets, ancient walls, gates, and temples, the incredibly colorful marketplace, and so many other sites Jesus knew. It was easy to see how His heart went out to this unique city as He said, "O Jerusalem, Jerusalem, thou that killest the prophets, and stonest them which are sent unto thee, how often would I have gathered thy children together, even as a hen gathereth her chickens under her wings, and ye would not!"

We traveled about Israel with our Bibles in hand, reading appropriate Scriptures aloud wherever we went. The beauty and lushness of the still-primitive land imprinted itself on our hearts. The rocks and desert reminded us of ascetic prophets, of Jesus' prayers and fasting. And we loved the everlasting, looming mountains, where time and again God revealed Himself to His chosen people.

Those physical, geographical places brought us very close to Jesus. The very stones of the earth reminded us we literally followed in His footsteps. And as we walked and prayed and read aloud from our Bibles, we began to know and understand Jesus as a Jew, and love his Jewishness.

Israelis love their land. They know God gave it to them. There's a sweetness and a vigor in these people, and it's so exciting to see what God is doing with Israel today. God's prophecies are being filled.

"When you see the dynamic faith alive in Israel today, you begin to see why these are God's people," Bob said. "You begin to understand why Jesus came down through that pure strain of people, the Tribe of Judah. Jesus followed all the Jewish laws as He was being raised, and this is where it all began. If it weren't for the Jews, if God had not punished them, then provided a way to salvation for the Gentiles, we all would be lost."

This fact hit us with real impact, day after day. As we found ourselves searching through unfamiliar bits of the Old Testament, the truth became clear: We did *not* know our Bible. Only through a knowledge and love of the Old Testament, we began to see, could we ever really begin to understand Jesus and His origin. And only then could we be able to witness to the Jews.

Incidentally, the Lord made a strange opportunity for me to witness to the Israelis the day our Conference opened. I felt honored to sing just before Prime Minister Ben-Gurion addressed the conference, and I chose "It Took a Miracle," "Amazing Grace," "I Walked Today Where Jesus Walked," and gave a few words of testimony. Ben-Gurion's remarks were broadcast over Israeli radio. Broadcast engineers were afraid the Christian songs preceding the prime minister's words might offend the Israelis, but there was no way they could successfully edit out the music.

Bob later learned my songs were the first Christian gospel music ever broadcast in the State of Israel. Christian music is aired, but it's Gregorian chants and other ancient music of the Roman Catholic Church. Before we left Israel several people commented that they had enjoyed my simple gospel songs, and I felt blessed that the Lord had let me witness in my small way to all the Israelis.

So God laid a burden on each of our hearts. We knew He had commissioned us to go home and begin learning for Him.

Faith. Jerusalem, the Holy City, sacred to three of the world's major faiths—Moslem, Jewish, Christian—literally has been built, shaped, changed, and preserved by Faith itself. Never before had any of us seriously considered what it would mean to be willing to die for our beliefs. The blood of believers has washed through Jerusalem streets over the centuries.

How would it feel to be stoned to death? At St. Stephen's Gate, where Stephen became the first Christian to be put to death for Christ's sake, you wonder. There—and so many other places—you come to realize how many Jews, Christians, and others have gone to their deaths for their beliefs.

Psalm 22:1–5 describes this absolute, imploring trust in God which you see again and again in modern Israel. This ancient song opens with the words Jesus quoted as He hung dying on the cross: "My God, my God, why hast thou forsaken me?"

Charlie and Marabel, Ron and Gloria, Bobby and Gloria, Bob and I, again and again returned to one special site: Gordon's Tomb, where scholars believe Jesus was buried. We worshipped there one morning, with the Reverend Roy McKuen, president of World Opportunities, Inc., leading the services. A relatively recent discovery, this place seems to bear all marks of authenticity. It is located just outside Jerusalem. There is the garden—the venerable olive trees, a large wine vat; there is Golgotha, the Place of the Skull, and—most heart-rending sight of all—the tomb.

To kneel and pray inside the tomb where Jesus was laid is an experience too profound to describe. The tomb itself is spacious, simple, well chiseled out of close-grained granite. The stone which sealed the entrance would have been rolled along a track, still perfectly usable. The Bible tells us the tomb was new, intended for Joseph of Arimathea, the rich man who placed Jesus' body there.

It's impossible to see the flat ledge on which He lay in death, to kneel on the hard, stony earth before it, and not be swept backwards in time, and feel part of that heartbreak. As you stand within the tomb's doorway, you realize this was where the angel stood. Just outside, a few paces beyond the door, would have stood the two Marys, blind with weeping. Beyond that spot, the gentle garden, its flowers, shrubs, and olive trees, must be much the same as it was during that long-ago first Easter. And beyond the whispering trees, at the crest of the hill, that horrifying place where they erected the cross.

We kept returning to Gordon's Tomb.

One day we were in a taxi with Ron and Gloria, Marabel and Charlie, our children, and Bob Walker, editor of *Christian Life*. As we rode to our hotel atop the Mount of Olives, we discussed the memorial our Conference proposed to give the city of Jerusalem. Delegates to the huge conference wished to donate a sound-and-light presentation to Gordon's Tomb. The idea dismayed Bob and me.

You see, virtually every inch of land significant to Christ's life on this earth over the centuries has been so adorned with gold, marble, and elaborate buildings, that man-made memorials obscure every other sacred site. Gordon's Tomb, because it is such a late discovery, has not fallen prey to man's passion for "improving" these holy places. There are no church buildings here, no shrines, no man-made adornments. Bob and I hated to think of adding anything at all to Gordon's Tomb.

Then the Holy Spirit gave Bob a wonderful idea. Several times Bob had commented that the one adverse thing about Gordon's Tomb was the overlook from Golgotha, the Place of the Skull, directly down into a noisy, Arab-owned bus station. The noisy motors and air pollution in such close proximity to that most sacred site appalled both of us.

"Wouldn't it be great if we of this conference could buy that property and give it to Gordon's Tomb?" Bob said. "How ideal if that could become the main entrance—if you could walk into a garden and look up towards Golgotha. That little piece of land could become a place of peace and rest, where the pilgrim could pause and feel the presence of God."

Everybody got very excited. When we got to our hotel we really prayed about it. And when the idea was presented to the committee in charge of choosing a memorial from the conference, they were very receptive. So was John Van Der Hooven, the warden of the Tomb, and also Mayor Teddy Kollek of Jerusalem.

It seems as though God is working. Bob is helping to set up a committee to accept contributions for this purpose. We don't want to erect a building of any sort—only a quiet, peaceful garden where the visitor can worship, pray, and meditate in preparation for coming to the Tomb where they laid our Lord.

It was in Jerusalem, as described in the second chapter of Acts, where the Holy Ghost appeared on the day of Pentecost to the ". . . Jews, devout men, out of every nation under heaven" (v. 5). Empowered by the Holy Spirit of God, these people were to institute the Church, the Body of Christ, of which all Christian believers are members.

When you journey to Jerusalem, it's to a city rich in the presence of the living God. No two Christians could experience Him the same way. But you find yourself right back there with Jesus' disciples as they asked Him, ". . . Lord, wilt thou at this time restore again the kingdom to Israel?" (v. 6).

Acts 1:7–8 gives His answer.

. . . It is not for you to know the times or the seasons, which the Father hath put in his own power.

But ye shall receive power, after that the Holy Ghost is come upon you: and ye shall be witnesses unto me both in Jerusalem, and in all Judaea, and in Samaria, and unto the uttermost part of the earth.

That Scripture, certainly after the overwhelming experience of walking where Jesus walked convicted Bob and me. We were to return to our country knowing God had commissioned us, too—and we cannot fulfill His commission until we learn His will. We must return to the Bible.

My mind flashes back to a picture of Charlie Morgan, tall and solemn, standing atop Mount Megiddo, reading Scriptures pertaining to the last battle of Armageddon, which will happen there.

The Bible is our only recourse. Jesus answered Satan's temptations with Scriptures. If we born-again believers would only learn the Bible as it is written, memorize it, and hold it in our hearts, this can be our only tool in overcoming the power of the devil. Jesus defeated the devil once and for all concerning the *guilt* of our sins by dying on the cross and rising again the third day.

I cling to Ephesians 6:11–20: "Put on the whole armour of God . . . ." If Christians would say that passage aloud every day, believe on it, act on it, the devil would become powerless in our lives. And one day, praise God, we will shed these bodies and the *presence* of sin will be a thing of the past. All Christians share that blessed hope.

Bob was right. Bobby and Gloria belonged with us during our life-changing days in Israel. Not only did our children glean far more than we'd dreamed they could from experiences which seemed to us too old for them, but also they saw their parents and other adults become worshipful, awed, literally thrilled by a new knowledge of God. They saw us seeking, truly yearning to know Jesus even better, and glorying in His reality.

Back home, there was almost no discussion about what would come next. We all just slid into a new life. A couple of times a week we'd come in from playing tennis—Marabel, Charlie, Bob and me—and without a suggestion, simply get our Bibles and sit around the dining-room table and discuss things we'd seen in Israel. Charlie got turned on by 2 Chronicles when he read it in The Living Bible (which really clarified and illuminated it). He and Bob would pore over that book by the hour, absorbed and excited.

Then God led those men into teaching a Sunday school class. In a way, you could hardly imagine anything so unlikely. Charlie used to be a very shy, conservative man; Bob always had been diffident about his faith.

Yes, Israel changed them. Obviously the trip to Jerusalem changed them both because they became so on fire for the Lord.

You don't have to go to Jerusalem—not in a literal sense, that is. But I saw, through our journey there, that each of us must go—in our hearts—to where we find Jesus, the one true, living God. We must go to our knees. We must go to our Bibles. Eventually, we may have to go to the "uttermost part of the earth." But we all need—we must have—the living God.

Bob and I urge you to make that pilgrimage. By all means go to Jerusalem if you can—Jerusalem the Holy City, Jerusalem the Golden.

But if you can't, you need go only so far as your closet. The important thing—the real pilgrimage—is to seek the living God. The outcome is certain, for Jesus Himself promised: "Seek and ye shall find . . ." (Matthew 7:17).

# 10

*Bob Green*

# The Lord's Business

I felt stymied. I had exhausted every means I knew, to go about getting a Christian secretary. This had been a burden to me for a long time. I just didn't see how I could put an ad in the paper asking for a called-apart girl who was Christian.

So I prayed. As so often happens in life, when all else fails, you turn to God. And when I prayed, Kathie Epstein's name popped into my head. I knew that was the answer.

"Bob, you know Kathie will be going to college," Anita said. She thought I was nutty. It wasn't likely she would be job-hunting. Anyhow, Anita thought I needed someone older—someone with work experience.

Though this made sense, it still didn't stop me. I phoned Kathie in Maryland and told her what was on my mind. We needed a secretary and she was qualified. When we talked to her parents, we learned they had misgivings about sending her to college and were praying about it. Our job offer seemed the answer to everybody's prayers.

So Kathie Epstein came to Villa Verde. She's smart, sweet, beautiful, and talented—and also something of a problem. You take an eighteen-year-old into your home and family— and things change. Kathie never before had been away from home. She had come to a new city, a new job, a totally different environment. She missed her close-knit family and her friends. In other words, she had adjustments to make.

And so did we. When we took on responsibility for this girl, our own "adopted" junior miss from Maryland, we got a preview of how it will be when our kids are of dating age. It's lively, okay?

Despite the necessary adjustments, I've known all along that Kathie is the answer. So much of our office work is of a religious nature. We're deluged with requests for Anita to sing and testify. It would be hard for a non-Christian secretary to deal with these people effectively. I felt sure Kathie had the Christian approach, as well as all the common sense and ability we could ask for.

Now, to back up a moment. I'd begun to realize there's a lot of difference between a Christian-who-is-a-businessman, and a Christian businessman. Little by little I had given over certain areas of my life to Christ. The business area probably was the last to go. As I said before, for a long time it didn't occur to me to pray about small problems and decisions in the office.

The Bible says we are to be "Not slothful in business; fervent in spirit; serving the Lord" (Romans 12:11). That's a high aim. Without prayer, it can't be accomplished.

So my praying for a secretary, and Kathie's coming down from Maryland, turned out to be a miracle far beyond anything Kathie, her parents, Anita, or I might have had in mind—because God had a plan for all of us.

Anita and I for years had been on the lookout for a talent—boy or girl—to help along. Nobody ever came along. At least, we never could get very excited over anybody who had talent who wasn't a Christian because we were very doubtful that anybody can make it in show business *per se* these days. But if you're a Christian and use your talent for the Lord—that's all you need.

Kathy Epstein's talent was something I immediately recognized at the Junior Miss Pageant. She has a beautiful voice, and sings sacred songs. We wanted to encourage her and help her develop this for the Lord.

Meanwhile, there was a backlog of requests for appearances which Anita couldn't possibly fill. I kept filing and saving them, wondering to myself, "Wouldn't it be great if I could find someone else to do this?"

Then Kathie came along. I realized she has a great testimony and a great voice—that she could do a lot of the things Anita didn't have time to do. At the same time, ministers from all over the country would phone me, asking me for Anita or some other Christian talent, to appear before their congregations. The scary thing was, they didn't know me at all except through Anita's books—yet they put their complete trust in my judgment. "Send us whoever you think . . . ," they'd say.

So we began sending Kathie out on a lot of the things Anita couldn't fit into her schedule. Kathie has been doing revivals all over the country, singing and testifying at State Baptist conventions, appearing at Youth for Christ rallies. And we began to understand why the Lord had put Kathie

Epstein's name in my mind. He meant us to help open some doors to her talent.

Gradually something new began to evolve. I began to feel the Lord wanted me to take what Kathie and I had begun, and expand it. The idea tantalized me; it stayed on my mind almost continually.

Show business has agents who book talent, but I had never heard of any large Christian agencies which could in any professional manner steer churches, revivals and the like toward talent. I saw a need for such an agency.

For example, how about the preacher in Oshkosh who only knows Christian performers by word of mouth. Where does he go? How does he get hold of somebody? It's easy to call Anita Bryant or Pat Boone or somebody like that, but how do you get hold of others—especially if you're a small church with a limited budget?

But I just kept the whole thing in my heart for a long time—just thought and prayed about it. I'm a cautious guy who doesn't leap into things fast. Finally I got around to mentioning it to Anita. She thought the idea was fantastic.

"A Christian talent agency? Oh, Bob, I *know* this is of the Lord," she said. "After all, now I am established. Our career is running smoothly. We've prayed for some new service for the Lord to come along for you—something that isn't Anita Bryant. I feel sure this is it. You're the only person I can think of who not only has the know-how but also sees the need, and is a born-again Christian."

I liked what she said, but there was one more point I needed to make. "Fine, Anita. But the thing is, I'm sure this won't be a money-making venture. Our agency fees will probably be absorbed by telephone charges alone. I'll do well to break even."

She didn't hesitate a minute.

"What does that matter, Bob? If the Holy Spirit gave you this idea, you're supposed to follow through. I believe this is the Lord's business!"

Fishers of Men Opportunities, Inc., thus came into being. And as it did, we added two other fine young girls to our professional and Christian family. Diane Graham is our pianist at Northwest Baptist Church. She is Kathie's age, an excellent pianist, wonderful with our children, and we're breaking her in to accompany Anita on some of her local church appearances. Gloria Roe, of course, is Anita's regular accompanist. Meanwhile Diane travels with Kathie as her accompanist. They make a fine little Christian team.

Recently we had to hire a girl to do nothing but write notes to people who are requesting Anita. Anita simply can't answer all these letters personally, but she does oversee the replies. Linda Carver, a girl from our church, helped with this for a while until she left to go into missionary work.

Then Rosemary Conner, a former Junior Miss from Alabama, joined us. Rosemary has become very valuable at our camp, fills in at home when Kathie Epstein has a booking, baby-sits, and has become like a sister to Kathie.

Through trial and error—with much prayer—our young staff has turned into quite a team. My choice of Kathie as secretary for a while seemed wrong. She didn't really like the work, didn't feel cut out for it, yet we all felt God had sent her to us.

Kathie, her parents, Anita, and I prayed for guidance. The answer was to hire Lynn Rothrum, a beautifully efficient secretary. Kathie then took over Anita's mail as her personal secretary, helps with the household staff, and is great with Fishers of Men Opportunities, Inc.

A significant thing about our new staff members is, they all came to us through prayer. Each girl is an outstanding

Christian with real talent, and beautiful character traits. Our children love them and they set our kids a great example. In addition, Michelle Epstein, Kathie's younger sister, has come down to pinch hit for Kathie occasionally. Michie, as the kids call her, also is great with children.

Fishers of Men Opportunities, Inc. has begun to move. Our agency will handle not only talent but Christian celebrities willing to give their testimonies—athletes, politicians, actors—anyone in the spotlight. It's not an exclusive agency. We'll book anyone on a nonexclusive basis. We'll make lists available and be like a clearing house. Churches, organizations, or groups who need speakers for one meeting or a week-long revival can get someone interesting.

If they want music we can give them Kathie, for example, or Gloria Roe. If they want a speaker we can give them Senator Mark Hatfield, or Col. Jim Irwin, the Apollo 15 astronaut, now retired from NASA to enter full-time Christian work—or maybe a local boy from their own state.

Our lists are far from complete; the Lord will add names as we grow.

"It's going to be difficult," I told Anita. "We're dealing with people who're not in the business. They know nothing about it so you have to do everything for them." It *is* difficult, but Kathie and I are getting it off the ground.

Two things struck home right away. First, working with Christians is something entirely different from the same work done out in the world. In the beginning, when I'd tentatively suggest Kathie as an alternative to Anita, the unknown pastor at the end of the long-distance line usually would say, "We'll take your word for it that Kathie is everything you say she is. Send her to us."

That kind of trust really got to me. It's refreshing. I discovered I could have a rapport with church people that

I ordinarily just wouldn't expect as a show-business agent. If there's any trouble about anything, I say, "I'll pray about it and you pray about it, and I'll call you back tomorrow." That's pretty heavy stuff!

Another thing I like is becoming a link between the church and the Christian who wants to witness. A lot of people I admire have agreed to be available to us for this: Mark Hatfield, a great American, Jim Irwin, the astronaut, and from the Miami Dolphins, such pro football players as Mike Kolen, Howard Twilley, and Norm Evans.

Take Norm Evans. He's a professional athlete and a man of God, and he's kept busy day and night. Norm has written a book. He is deluged with requests for him to give his Christian testimony.

First of all, Norm doesn't know how to handle this sort of thing. He needs someone to guide him. For me, setting up air-line and hotel reservations, having him met at the plane, is almost second nature. It's not work to me, but for him it is. If people like Norm have someone who can do all this, set everything up, arrange the right publicity, it's just that much off their back. It's a real satisfaction to me both as a Christian and as a businessman to serve as that link.

On the other hand, I came to see my original vision of a Christian talent agency had some naïve aspects. In the show-business world, it's all strictly business: very standard, very cut and dried. In the church, I was to learn, business arrangements often can be surprisingly cloudy and vague.

From my observations (comparing the business field to the sacred), we Christians sometimes come out far behind. I think we're really in competition with non-Christians. We need to start upgrading our Christian worth. In order to do that, we must become more professional, and begin to handle things on a much higher plane.

I was surprised to see how much infighting exists in the Christian world, for example, and how many misunderstandings arise from these vague verbal contractual arrangements. Kathie has been taken great advantage of when a church asks her to do one thing, then puts her through an entire day of "working for the Lord." She doesn't mind this, but it's still unfair. The planned projects should be understood ahead of time. That's simple love and consideration.

Sometimes a church brings Kathie into a city, pays her transportation, and there's no guarantee of a fee. There's a love offering—which may be fine—or may be nothing. If other local churches also want her, the church which sponsored her blows its top; they don't want any other church in town to have her!

Now these are Christians, but I think their attitude is not right. They are being denominational, not universal Christians. We're talking about spreading the gospel of Jesus Christ, and that should involve no competition. If Kathie went to another church and even one person heard the gospel because of her, every church in town should rejoice.

The Apostle Paul told us about "speaking the truth in love" (Ephesians 4:15), and I offer these observations in that spirit. I believe handling church arrangements in a more businesslike way for the Lord will help more people witness for Jesus. It's not that people are turned off by lack of money, or love offerings, but by the lack of honesty, the cloudy and vague way arrangements are made.

So I began—cautiously—to feel my way along in this very new business. I felt like a trail blazer. Consulting with ministers, church officials, evangelists, and other Christians who regularly travel about America giving their testimonies, I discovered wide variations in the way these people are treated.

For example, churches seem willing to pay a set fee for a star, but not for lesser personalities. Anita never charges a fee for work in the sacred field. The Lord has blessed us, and this is one of our ways of tithing.

Still, with someone like Anita, churches always ask what financial arrangements must be made. They know someone of her standing expects a fee, not an honorarium. So they expect to pay someone like Anita Bryant—yet they give a token (on the other hand) to some poor evangelist with five children to support—a full-time Christian worker.

This turns me off. I see nothing in the Scriptures that would indicate it's wrong to establish an agreed-upon fee ahead of time—or anything to indicate love offerings are better. The more I consulted with ministers over America, with evangelists and others, and the more I prayed about it, the more convinced I became that too many of us Christian businessmen practice better business for ourselves than we do for the Lord.

Evangelists should not have to negotiate fees nor worry about compensation. Nor should they have to sell books, records, and tapes in the church vestibule in order to augment a skimpy love offering. To plug books and records from the pulpit, it seems to me, dilutes a man's testimony. Too often we put our men of God in the position of turning God's house into a marketplace.

Fees are *not* the issue here, you realize: *Christian business dealings are.* We decided our agency will offer a range of people in all categories and price brackets. We let the individual decide his fee, based on how far he travels, value of his time away from home, and that sort of thing. We believe clear-cut advance understandings will free everyone from problems. It will eliminate money-counting at the height of a revival, and will keep the pulpit from becoming commercial.

But if these celebrities are such great Christians, some will ask, why must they speak for money? The answer is, anything any of us has to give requires our time. The church which offers an athlete a fee to speak helps him give of himself, perhaps, to a church which can't afford any fee. When you average your work for the Lord, it will balance out.

Also, the speaker who works for the Lord is, after all, a steward of whatever money he receives. No one should begrudge him his fee but assume he'll use it as a Christian—responsibly.

These questions are delicate ones. We pray as we go, realizing we're dealing with like-believers, and God will lead us in our decisions. For my part, there's a challenge to learning and operating within the business area of the Christian faith. Until a few months ago, I had no idea about most of it. As the Lord leads us, I've begun to believe He wants to put my particular know-how to work. That's pretty exciting.

These days, when a difficult phone call comes in, I send up a quickie prayer. It really helps. Sometimes I talk to preachers who get somewhat bugged on the phone. I know I've already prayed about our conversation before we started talking. I can hear from *their* end of the line that they did not pray about it, or their attitudes would be different.

I admit the idea of praying about business dealings is something new in my life. Prayer has revolutionized my business habits and attitudes. When you go into partnership with Christ—things change.

It's interesting to speculate how much the world could change if the average businessman would open up his office to Jesus. One thing, he'll discover talents and abilities within himself he didn't know he had. He'll learn Christ wants to use these. Another thing, the Lord's business livens up your life. You never know what He plans to do next. The unexpected continually happens. Adventure always is just around the corner!

This summer we're trying something new. We've been led to form the Anita Bryant Summer Camp for girls eight to sixteen, using the facilities of Bibletown in Boca Raton, Florida. We'll offer a full curriculum, with a spiritual approach—a sort of junior version of Marabel Morgan's "Total Woman" concept. We're interested in girls who have talents to develop, and we'd like to be able to guide them in this.

Again, it's a new avenue toward what God seems to want us to do. We never know where He'll take us next or what unexpected thing we may try. You just have to hang loose.

The main thing is to remember it's the Lord's business— and not your own. He has given you everything you have. He also gives the responsibility of stewardship. In 2 Timothy 2:15, Paul says, "Study to shew thyself approved unto God, a workman that needeth not to be ashamed, rightly dividing the word of truth."

And in 1 Corinthians 3:8, 9 he tells us,

> Now he that planteth and he that watereth are one; and every man shall receive his own reward according to his own labour.
> For we are labourers together with God: ye are God's husbandry, ye are God's building.

I don't say it's easy. Sometimes decisions are hard to make. Mistakes seem to abound, and things get tough. Also, you discover you're working harder for the Lord than you ever did for yourself!

Still, I never heard any man say he regretted going into partnership with Jesus. God is not the author of confusion— or failure. The day you decide to take the Lord's business seriously is the day you get serious about life.

With Jesus your work is the same and your risks are the same—and yet, somehow they're not—because *you* aren't the same. The Christian businessman is a transformed man.

As Paul in Romans 8:31, also tells us, "If God be for us, who can be against us?"

# 11

# Building a Christian Home

A Christian home never comes about by accident. I believe it must require more grace and hard work than any other organization on earth.

Bob and I receive letters every day from Americans who express deep yearnings and real concern for the quality of life in their homes. They know they need God in their lives. They want God in their children's lives. How do you find this? they ask us. Where do you begin?

To establish a Christian home, you must begin with the individuals in it. More accurately, you must start with yourself—wherever you are, whatever your role.

The initial step is to make sure your own relationship to God is right by accepting His Son, Jesus Christ, as your personal Lord and Saviour. Nothing else can happen until you do. But when that right relationship is established, *anything* can happen. I mean it. We get so many letters telling about miracles that happened within four walls of a home. You can only praise Jesus for them!

However, a "good" home never will be good enough.

If you read Romans 5:12 and Romans 5:19 you have your answer to those who claim they're morally good, don't lie, steal, or commit other obvious sins. Again, Romans 6:23 states our dilemma very plainly and tells what we can do about it. And in Romans 10:9 God gives us very specific instructions as to our personal salvation.

There it is in black and white—clear directions from God. Also, there's the tremendous promise that "whosoever shall call upon the name of the Lord shall be saved" (v. 13).

How *impossible* it is to be a wife *unless* you have been born again. Only by the grace of God can any human relationship be perfected. Without God's grace, most marriages prove unbearable—the present divorce rate proves that!

Nowadays many intelligent young women attempt to establish good homes on mere social and psychological precepts. They turn to the well-meaning advice you find in popular magazines. I don't knock it. Much of it is good. However, it never goes far enough. It will leave you stranded every time. If you truly are serious about life, nothing short of Jesus can suffice.

How can you be born again? Christ tells us in John 3:1–21. The story of Nicodemus is one of the most beautiful in the Bible. "Born again," of course, is the same as being saved.

Once you're born again you immediately have a hot line to heaven. It's important to begin talking daily to God through prayer and to have God talk to you through reading His Word. Ask Jesus daily to take over every facet of your life. God is not concerned with eloquent words. He cares about what you say, not how you say it. And after you're born again, Jesus gives you a magnificent promise in Luke

12:8: ". . . Whosoever shall confess me before men, him shall the Son of man confess before the angels of God."

As new born-again Christians we must in obedience to God become baptized, as taught in Colossians 2:12. It's important to choose a Bible-believing church—one that teaches the pure Word of God. Christ instituted His church as a place where we can confess our sins one to another, bear one another's burdens, and where a man of God can furnish leadership to his flock.

Many people consider all this too old fashioned and simple. They think it so unsophisticated as to be irrelevant to life in today's America. Nevertheless, Americans are hungering and searching for the Word, without even knowing what they seek. They want *reality*. Only Jesus Christ can supply that.

Nobody can be adequately involved at home until he's first involved in church. It's so important not to marry outside of your faith—outside of the church. That's one of the biggest problems some families face today.

However, even if you did marry a nonbeliever, God still can supply your deepest needs. Many a woman blames her marital problems on her nonbelieving husband—yet refuses to ask God to help their situation. As the believer, she should turn *first* to Jesus.

God's first instruction to wives is that we must love our husbands. A wife must keep her place. If she nags that husband to go to church, if she puts him down—she disobeys God's instructions.

On the other hand, where the woman and children can be faithful to God and His church without turning the husband off, there's much hope. If a husband allows his wife freedom to attend church, she should—by all means—be faithful. Commit the husband to constant prayer and set a

Christian example before him. That means a *loving* example.

After all, few of us start out with ideal marital situations. God can take us *where we are today*, however, and change the whole picture. He can work miracles in any home—unless *we* place obstacles before Him.

This reminds me of something in my life I'm ashamed to admit—a problem involving money.

I believe Christian families should tithe. Before marriage I always tithed my income without thinking twice about it because to me it seems such a natural part of Christian discipline. On the other hand, I never managed money wisely. Bob soon learned I was like a child where finances are concerned, but fortunately he is wiser than I in that respect. With the expert help of Phil Braunstein, Bob managed our funds.

So we rocked along for years, apparently very well, except that Phil and Bob's attitudes toward tithing differed from mine. "Look, Anita, you can put a definite value on your services. You never charge a fee for giving your services to churches. That's part of your tithe," they said. "Besides, the Green family gives very generously of its dollars. Nobody could possibly criticize you."

In a way, they were very convincing. I knew they were totally sincere in their attitudes. I also knew that if we added the value of our appearances for the Lord to the actual dollars we gave, we'd more than tithe. Still, I didn't feel right about it.

"Jesus said, 'For where your treasure is, there will your heart be also.' " I told them. "Nowhere in the Bible does God tell us to tithe off the bottom—after taxes, and so on."

We never could seem to agree on that point, so I prayed about it. Convinced as I was that we should give God 10 percent off the top of our income, I knew also that I could not demand this. Bob's efforts as well as mine are represented in our income. We had to agree. He would have to want to tithe.

I did a lot of nagging about it. Also, as soon as the twins came, I started nagging Bob and Phil to add a wing to our house—a very necessary expense, in my opinion. "Anita, the architect's estimate runs as much as we paid for our previous house," Bob said. "There's just no way we can do it modestly. I think we should put it off for a while."

His manner was quiet and definite. Underneath, unspoken, ran a certain current of hostility. I knew what he was thinking. *If you weren't so extravagant, Anita, we could do it.*

Well, I was determined we *would* do it. So determined, in fact, that I consented to something I hate—a financial conference with Bob and Phil Braunstein. I'd tell Phil we had to have the addition to our house. Also, I'd inform them it was time for our family to tithe our dollars.

What an ordeal! It had been years since I actually had looked at facts and figures, and the truth was brutal. There was the evidence of my shopping sprees—especially clothes for the children and me. I'm utterly undisciplined where clothes are concerned—and gifts—and spending of that type.

"You see, Anita, you're not buying too many luxuries like furs, designer originals, jewels, and so on, but you're still spending fantastic sums on ordinary purchases." Phil said. The figures he showed me were absolutely horrifying.

I felt so terrible, but Bob and Phil didn't rub it in. Instead, they tried to open my eyes as gently as possible. "Now that you see the picture, you understand," Bob said. "Building costs are just too high now."

"We have to!" I stubbornly insisted.

Phil and Bob looked at one another helplessly.

"Well, then, which means more to you?", Bob challenged. "Shall we add to the house—or tithe?"

"Both!", I said, angrily.

"You can't have both."

"Tithe, then!" I said unhesitatingly. My answer caught both men by surprise.

"Anita!" Phil protested. "Do you know how much that is in dollars?"

"Yes, Phil, but I don't care. The federal government certainly taxes us off the top. Our agent's percentage comes off the top. Your percentage is off the top. So why should God's tithe come out of what's left over?

"Look, Phil, I'll make a deal. If in six months this doesn't work out, I'll be the first to tell you God is a liar. I'll come and say there's nothing to His Word. *I promise.*"

Phil shot me a quick grin, then shook his head. "We both know better than that," he said gently. We walked toward the door. "How do you feel about this, Bob?" Phil asked.

"Maybe this will make Anita wake up to her spending habits," Bob said thoughtfully.

Once again, I had blamed Bob's spiritual deficiencies instead of my own. It was hard to admit how immature and wrong I had been about the use of money. Also, I thought Bob just arbitrarily refused to tithe. I had criticized him constantly—yet wouldn't look at my own share of the blame. Indeed, I wouldn't even let him discuss money with me!

Days later, as we rode to church, Bob again brought up the subject of tithing—eagerly, this time. "Do you know what I'd like us to do? We could support a missionary family, Anita. We could really increase our church's bus ministry . . . ." On and on his ideas flowed. And when I glanced toward my husband, there were tears in his eyes.

So, where born-again Christians work and pray together, the Holy Spirit will convict each one of his failings—and Christ will help us change.

Even in terrible home situations, there still can be hope. Sometimes a man actually forbids a woman to attend church or to instruct their children. Nevertheless, if she remains faithful to her husband as God tells her to be, and if she is truly born again and prays for God to right their situation, He will honor her faith.

First of all, however, He expects her to obey her husband. Then she must commit him and all their circumstances to prayer, for she of herself can change nothing. Unless she has great faith there can be no solution, and she will lapse into resentment. With faith, however, her Christian example could change the husband's heart.

Jesus helps us when we have the faith to pray. Being born again comes from above. We have to ask for it.

The Bible says, "God setteth the solitary in families . . ." (Psalms 68:6). Most of us truly are babes in Christ—if indeed we are in Christ at all—when first we set out to form a family structure. Lucky is the couple who lives by the Word of God from the outset. For the rest of us, what a marvelous day when we adopt God's Word as our permanent guide!

Bob and I look to Ephesians 5:21–33 as our basic instructions as to what God expects of man and wife. Ephesians 6:2–4 concerns children. The discipline of that Scripture is not necessarily that of America's most famous pediatrician, but nevertheless it works.

God says children must be taught obedience and discipline. Anything worthwhile requires effort on the parents' part. Children need the security of parental authority as described in the Bible—authority administered with patience and love.

Today's young generation has grown up for the most part

with too little loving discipline. These young people often say their parents hate them. The Bible would bear the kids out, for it says the father who doesn't chasten his son, hates his son (Proverbs 13:24). Children somehow know this. They know it takes more love and hard work to discipline them.

Brother Bill Chapman, our pastor, says God would have made us like sea turtles—to lay our eggs in the sand, then return to the sea and let them hatch by themselves—if that's what He intended in the way of human nurturing. As mothers, we need to care for our children ourselves. I think I was miserable within myself when I was not totally caring for my children. I had a biological need to do it.

Obedience is the first law of the universe, Brother Bill also emphasizes. In nature itself, in one's education or job, wherever you meet life head-on, you have to conform to the universe. If we were left to run amok in accordance with each individual will, what a chaotic and violent world we would create!

Proverbs 19:18 tells us to "Chasten thy son while there is hope. . . ." That's interesting, because it takes note of the fact that there comes the time when there is no hope. That verse continues, ". . . And let not thy soul spare for his crying."

Sometimes we parents become victims of our guilt feelings, and slack up on our children's discipline. We can't do this to them! More and more our world offers temptations to lead these children seriously astray. Our only recourse as parents is to stick to the Word of God and use His outline (as given in the Bible) for training and loving them.

If we follow God's Word we have a promise our children will turn out all right. The Bible says, "Train up a child in the way he should go: and in his old age he will not depart from it" (Proverbs 22:6).

*In his old age* is the key to that verse. He may depart in adolescence, may rebel and do stupid things, but God promises he will *return*. Bob and I are trying to train our children in God's way so we won't have to fear problems with adolescence, or anything else that may come later.

"You can fool Mommy and Daddy," we tell our kids. "We don't know what's in your heart. But God knows everything." We want them to know God primarily as love, but also to realize we're all accountable for every idle word we utter. When they leave home they can put away their parents' commandments—but they can't cast off God's commandments.

Brother Bill cautions that a child reared in a strict religious sense—but denied love—will rebel. He warns that there's a real danger in drumming religion into your kids—mere rules and regulations—unless you're willing to live out God's desires before them. If a child doesn't see Jesus in his home he will become disillusioned with so-called Christians and the established church.

We all have doubts about whether or not we're doing right. You can always get advice from friends and relatives, and the so-called experts. Most reassuring of all, however, is the fact that we can clarify every doubt by turning to the Word of God. That is our Source, and we must respect, revere, and live up to it in our homes. If we don't live it, it has no meaning.

If we rely on Jesus, we can be sure of how our children will grow up. One thing—we don't have a permissive God. Someone has said that if God wanted His children reared permissively, He'd have given Moses the Ten Suggestions!

Another thing, why don't we let children *be* children? Why must they grow up so soon?

Bob and I with Gloria and Ron Robertson were watching

a TV news documentary concerning riots at Berkeley University. After a thoughtful discussion of the situation, the narrator closed with a provocative comment about some of today's young people: "The problem with youth today is that they want to teach before they learn, retire before they work, and rot before they ripen." Cynical as that sounds, there may be some small element of truth in it.

Obviously building a Christian home requires day-to-day effort. Unless you're working at *con*structing, in fact, the devil probably is working at *de*structing. Recently in New Members' class we discussed how the devil undermines us. Brother Bill asked, "Does the devil go for your weaker points —or the stronger ones?"

Immediately I said I thought he aims for our weaknesses.

"No, just the opposite," Bob said. "He heads for the strongest points because then he's got you—the whole kaboodle."

"That's right," Brother Bill agreed. "But we must be mindful that we have *no* strong points where the devil is concerned. If we think we do, we're already defeated. Our one defense against him is to put on the whole armor of God."

That's why serious home-builders must begin each day with Bible reading and prayer. This is our armor. It is all we have and all we need.

"Pray as if everything depended upon God and work as if everything depended on you," Bob once told his Sunday-school class. If we don't read and dig into the Word—if we fail to seek God in prayer—we're the ones who miss out on the blessings. It's not easy. We have to put forth much effort, but the rewards are eternal.

Perhaps all this sounds terribly serious. It *is*.

Bob and I, so deeply in love, twelve years ago founded a family. We thought we were old enough, serious enough, to know what we were doing. Today, all these years later, we realize we're just now getting started—in the sight of God.

Despite any number of false starts and failures, however, one thing is sure. When we trust ourselves to Jesus, He leads. He honors our faith. That promise is big enough for any family—no matter how bogged down it may be at this moment.

Maybe your family needs a new start. So many times we have! If so, ask God to help you. He will answer that prayer. Today sometimes our friends who are not born-again believers say they see something in our family they wish they had. We are happy. Our children are cheerful, happy people.

"Jesus gets all the credit," Bob and I are quick to say. Without Him, we have nothing.

Bob and I have come to know the most wonderful personal testimony in the world still must be measured in these common, ordinary terms. Is your home happy? Are your children right with God? Do you and your husband have a good relationship?

The answers should be *yes*. Certainly all these things—and much more—can be yours—through the love of Jesus Christ.

# 12

# The Greatest Gift

The greatest gift God gave married couples is *not* sex. It is love. It's the totally honest, unselfish, in-depth love any of us would give literally anything in this world to experience.

*Does he really love me?* When a woman asks herself that question she's not thinking of sexual satisfaction but of much, much more. She's thinking of the overwhelming, pure love you encounter, for example, in Genesis 29:20:

> And Jacob served seven years for Rachel; and they seemed unto him but a few days, for the love he had to her.

Imagine such love! Every married couple in the world must crave it. Where two people build their home on Christian principles, the highest kind of love can exist. And it's in that context—the beauty of something God-given—that a couple's sex life should be established.

Christian sex has everything. First, it's legal—entered into through marriage, according to God's purposes—sanctioned by God Himself.

Married sex, as with all else God created, is beautiful. Read the Song of Solomon—that poem of pure delight. Here the Bible describes some of the thrilling emotions a man can feel toward a woman—a woman toward her man.

Best of all, Christian sex is total. It involves not just the physical but the whole person—body, soul, and spirit. And unless two people can give themselves to one another in the completeness God intends, no amount of mere sexual expertise will ever wholly satisfy.

Pick up almost any magazine today, and you'll find an article purporting to help you find sexual "fulfillment." Some of them include excellent information, no doubt—as far as they go. But placing a physical emphasis on sex is such a small part of the whole.

The rest includes the more subtle aspects of your relationship; the harmony two people create, the trust and caring between them, things that make them laugh, delight shared in things of the mind and spirit. God means you and your mate to have all this, and more.

A couple's sex life can be something of a barometer as to their marital weather report. If sex communications are poor, that's a serious symptom of more important problems. Experts agree that disharmony in sex usually precedes divorce. It can be a real warning signal.

I suppose every marriage in the world has sex difficulties at times, however. Usually these stem from something else. A drastic change in our situation (my taking over care of the twins) brought Bob and me to this place. Mental and physical fatigue just plain got to us. We reached a point where we didn't bother even to kiss goodnight.

It kept bugging me that Bob didn't hold my hand or kiss me goodnight, but I was too proud to mention it. Besides, maybe some of it was my fault. I'd get pretty uptight when I got overtired, and then I'd say a few sharp words to him.

You can't rock along that way too long, though. Lack of communication is dangerous, and I knew it. I recalled that Marabel advocates, when things get stale, wearing something really different and seductive and meeting your husband at the door when he comes home from work.

Well, I couldn't do that! Bob works right here at home. He's in and out all the time. I never meet him at the door. However, we were scheduled to make an appearance in Texas. Why couldn't I turn that trip into a mini-honeymoon? So I went to my favorite clerk at one of my favorite stores and asked her to show me the sexiest peignoir set she had.

"I have a heavy date," I told her. She gave me a strange look. "With my husband," I added hastily.

I felt lucky to find such a stunning gown and peignoir. Hot pink. *Perfect,* I thought. I began to feel pleased about my little conspiracy with myself. Before we left for Houston I managed to squeeze in everything else I wanted, too—manicure, pedicure, massage, hairdo. By the time Bob and I caught the plane, me with my fancy new pretties safely packed, I felt good about the way things were going.

(Little did I know.)

"Turn your watch back an hour," Bob reminded me on the plane. He's the one who keeps up with time zones and details like that. All I have to do is go. Well, I didn't change my watch—which turned out to be my *first* mistake.

Our plane arrived in Houston a few minutes early. The limousine scheduled to meet us at the airport had not shown up. Since I didn't like standing around, I began insisting that Bob get us a taxi. He refused.

"No, we'll wait for the limousine," he said. "It wouldn't be fair to stand him up just because our plane got in early." I knew Bob was right but I didn't like it. I'd begun to worry about my performance, and wanted to get to the hotel. Every minute counted. I began to stew. By the time the limousine arrived, I'd said a few mean things.

At the hotel, Bob asked me to have lunch with him. My temper snapped.

"Bob, that's a big time waster. There goes another hour— for nothing. Why don't you eat on the plane like I do?"

I knew why, of course. Bob was watching his diet pretty carefully and wanted to order his choice of lunch. But I didn't choose to sit with him while he ate. Instead I went on up to our room.

Then something occurred to me. "The flight!", I said to myself. "Good heavens, we'll have to get up at five o'clock tomorrow morning to catch our plane!" Naturally, that didn't fit in with my plans, so that put me in an even worse mood.

By the time Bob got upstairs I was fuming. I told him to change our next day's reservations to a later flight.

"Why?" he asked. "You made a point of insisting on the early flight. Said you wanted to hurry back to the kids. What's up?"

I didn't explain. Instead, I just started griping about everything else. By now Bob's temper was rising. He gave me a cold stare. "Why don't you pray about it, Anita?"

His sarcasm made me really mad. "Look, Bob, I don't have time for all this. You've been horsing around with lunch, and we've got a show to do. Time is getting away."

Another cold stare. Then, quietly, "Is that so! Did you set your watch back like I told you, Anita?"

Silence. Of course I had not. Bob saw he had me, and he

didn't yield at all. A stern look came over his face. "There's plenty of time," he said deliberately. "You know perfectly well I keep track of the time. I always do."

Considerably chastened, I calmed down. We did the show. Despite all our hassles, I realized the Lord still can use you even when you're having difficulties with your husband. I witnessed to several people backstage. This made me feel better.

Back at the hotel, a successful show behind us, my mood began to lift. When Bob told me he'd changed our flight from seven A.M. to eleven the next morning, I felt quite pleased. So I drifted out, feeling a rare sense of leisure, and took my time primping and dressing up in my new finery. At last I drifted back *in*—and it must have been the flattest grand entrance in history.

He just looked. (It was a very unimpressed look.)

"Is that one of those I bought you for Christmas?" he asked.

"No."

He turned away. That was that. You can imagine my feelings. Bob didn't say anything else at all, and I felt too crushed to speak to him. I tried to pray. Bob made no further mention, took absolutely no notice. He simply went to bed without a word.

So I sat up until midnight doing needlepoint—in quite a state. I alternated between grief and fury. What was wrong? I felt rejected, disappointed, and worried. I had been so excited about spending an evening together just by ourselves. I really needed him, and had gone to so much trouble just for him. I almost *hated* Bob for not responding to all that trouble I went to.

So I put all the blame on him. It didn't occur to me to blame that most harmful member of my body—the tongue.

That was what turned him off, and no amount of anything else could have turned him on. However, I didn't realize any of that, that night. I was furious!

The next morning Bob called home. He had to cancel tennis and make several other changes in plans. He'd changed the flight just to shut me up, I thought, feeling terribly sorry for myself. He returned to the bedroom, and we still weren't talking. There was coolness and strain between us. I felt miserable. We might just as well have taken that early flight, the way *he* acted, I thought.

Then, to make matters worse (and I thought they couldn't be worse!), we got a phone call saying our eleven o'clock flight had been canceled. There wouldn't be another until one o'clock that afternoon. Bob had to phone home again and make still more changes in plans. By now he was hostile to me.

"This should teach me something," he said tersely. "From now on when I do something, I'll stick to it and not let you change my mind."

He was really fuming. I felt sort of sick. As I sat there, the Holy Spirit convicted me that the whole mess was my own doing. And Bob continued to rave.

"Anita, you chose the early flight time," he reminded me. "You insisted on it. Then you insisted that I change it, with no word of explanation. And now you're trying to blame all this mess on me!"

He was mad. There wasn't much I could say. I took a deep breath. "You're right, Bob. It's all my fault, and I apologize."

"I accept your apology. It *is* all your fault. All of this headache for nothing, and your complaining about little things."

I decided to level with him. "The reason was—I was disappointed. I went out and bought this beautiful peignoir and you took one look and said, 'Did I get you that for Christmas!' "

"Sure," he said. "I was still mad at you for all the complaining you had done. I didn't turn on because I knew it was supposed to turn me on."

I felt totally chagrined. The truth hurts. By this time I was really humble. "What does turn you on?" I asked.

Silence for a moment. Then another direct, stern look.

"Kindness, Anita."

I felt terrible. I realized it all was of my own doing. I had not had the right spirit with Bob to begin with. I wasn't letting him make decisions. I wasn't upholding him as head of our household. I felt about half an inch high, and very close to tears.

When I could talk, I apologized. I asked Bob to forgive me, and of course he did. And then we had real closeness in every way. After all, kindness did turn him on!

Back home, I confided this little experience to Marabel. "Anita, what Bob said really rings a bell with me," she said. "Read Proverbs 31:10–31 in The Living Bible translation."

When I read that it made me want to cry. I realized how wrong I had been, and how it had affected Bob's love for me, and our sex life. When you can honor your husband as the Bible tells you to do, and hold him up as God wants you to, all other things will fall into place within the relationship.

When you're loving your husband as you should, it will come back to you, not only in kindness and other ways, but also in your sex life. That's why so many gals are so frustrated and unhappy these days—not from an inadequate sex life but because they're basically not what God says the wife should be to the husband.

That experience really taught me a lesson. Since then I strive, by praying about it, to remember what Christ wants of me. Whether Bob's judgment is right or wrong, in my estimation, I take it as from the head of our household. When he asks my opinion, I give it gladly. But I let him make the decisions now. He is head of our house.

Even at this stage of our marriage, when we've had so many other hurdles to surmount, this still is a great problem. Submission is, I mean—the idea of turning all leadership over to Bob. Still, I know the worth of any marriage only comes in proportion to the trust between man and woman.

I like what Ruth Stafford Peale wrote on this subject: "A man's job, basically, is to tame the world; a wife's job is to control herself—and indirectly her husband."

Loving trust, of course, is essential to a good sex relationship. In a newspaper interview, Dr. Mary S. Calderone, director of the Sex and Education Council of the United States, a noted authority on human sexuality, said sex shouldn't be required to carry the full burden of marital satisfaction. Equally important, she said, is the development of true intimacy in marriage, based on trust. This happens gradually "until the two people are no longer afraid to be vulnerable with each other."

In turn, this leads to a "real sense of delight in the relationship." Distorting the importance of physical aspects of marriage, according to Dr. Calderone, can result in serious complications.

The Bible supports her observations. If you want to become a lover (and not a sex object) the Bible tells you how. Chapter 13 of 1 Corinthians is something every one of us wives could read profitably every day. It might keep us on course—keep us from becoming as self-centered as I was in Houston.

One lesson I'm learning, in obedience, in not complaining and fussing, is that your relationship to your husband really is as unto Christ, and that you just must trust him. You must trust him even at those times when it seems things are going badly, and not the way you'd have them. Somehow they do work out for your good.

Bob isn't perfect, but he looks out for my good because he loves me. He wants the best for me. He certainly will make mistakes, but overall he simply wants to please me and make me happy.

I learned this last year when Bob booked us on our anniversary. I didn't say too much about that because it was a Billy Graham Crusade—which I believe in so much. After that, though, Bob had arranged for us to fly directly to the islands to do a business booking—which seemed a bit too much.

I was upset the whole time. He didn't mention our anniversary. There were no flowers in our room. He gave me some jewelry, but there was no romantic deal like I thought there should be. There again, it was what *I* thought it should be instead of what Bob might have planned.

Our whole day disappointed me. But what I didn't know was that Bob had made reservations for us for a four-day second honeymoon in Puerto Rico. It wasn't a booking at all, but a beautiful, sentimental surprise.

Unfortunately, my selfish attitude and glum behavior had killed all his pleasure in surprising me.

So this year I played it cool when he booked us on my birthday at Atlantic City. I was right to keep quiet. Not only had Bob not forgotten the date, but the beautiful bracelet he gave me almost took my breath away. It matches earrings he gave me on another anniversary.

This last instance taught me again that I must uphold him

in the things he does—not so I'll be rewarded with jewelry and romantic trips, but so I'll not miss something that really is beyond price—Bob himself.

God has sanctioned our marriage, and the Holy Spirit dwells within Bob. The Lord expects Bob to take charge of our household, and for me to uphold him in his decisions. This is what I must do, according to the Word of God.

Ruth Graham, the evangelist's wife, says, "I really believe God's directives are that our husbands are the head of the home. We adjust ourselves to them, not the other way around. That is why I tell young girls who are planning to get married, to marry a man they won't mind adjusting to. I realize there have to be mutual adjustments, but I am talking about the overall picture. The burden of the adjustments rests on the wife—or should."

Where love is, there can be a thrillingly beautiful sex relationship. God has planned it this way. Despite all of today's frankness about sex, however, despite the new so-called freedom, new knowledge, new research on the subject, I just don't believe sex in itself—without love and commitment—can have full beauty. Certainly it would have very little meaning.

God intends for men and women to delight in the physical as well as other aspects of their lives together. Certainly Christian partners can adjust where sexual difficulties arise. There are doctors, clinics, counselors to help with physical or emotional problems concerning sex. And there is prayer and the Bible to guide man and wife into a greater knowledge of what God expects of them as individuals, partners, and lovers.

The secret of love, of course, is *giving*. Someone has said that sex begins at the breakfast table, and I agree. It's a network of all the small things a couple does, says and is together—the caring and sharing, honesty and closeness, mistakes and forgiveness, laughter, encouragement, obedience, and trust.

In 1 John 4:7–21, you'll find wonderful insights into what love is and can be. Among other things, this passage advises, "Perfect love casteth out fear" (v. 18). In a relationship that's merely physical, fear can and almost surely will exist as one partner attempts to hold the other through sexual attraction.

The born-again Christian, however, does not have to fear. His love is of God, and therefore he can afford to trust. He can trust his partner, because he first trusts the Son of God—Jesus!

As Paul says in 1 Corinthians 13:13, "And now abideth faith, hope, and charity, these three; but the greatest of these is charity [love]."

Love is God's greatest gift. All else follows.

# 13

*Bob Green*

# Husbands, Love Your Wives

"Try praising your wife, even if it does frighten her at first," Billy Sunday once said.

Well, I might be able to overlook that. But recently Brother Bill Chapman, our respected minister, has been socking it to us on the same subject.

"There's a woman in your house," he said. "The Lord made her to be fulfilled by love. She's married to you, so she's out of it so far as the world's concerned. She's off-limits.

"Nobody else in the universe, in heaven or hell, can love your wife—except you. You must not leave any question—any doubt—in the mind of that woman. Then that house won't be a prison for her but a palace."

Brother Bill, as Anita has mentioned, doesn't just preach; he practices what he preaches. He has said the Lord well may judge him even more as husband and father than as minister of the gospel. I wonder how many other men would look at it that way.

Where do a man's first duties lie, anyhow? In Christian service? Business? Community affairs? Making a living? To our wives and children?

Consciously or unconsciously, a man sorts out his priorities in life. Maybe if more men were to move their wives closer to the top of that priority list, it might reflect in lowered national divorce rate figures.

"Husbands, love your wives," Brother Bill said. He was quoting from the Bible. (He'd had us open our Bibles to Ephesians 5:25.) "Husbands, love your wives, even as Christ also loved the church, and gave himself for it."

Fortunately, Anita and I took a tape recorder to New Members' Class that night. We didn't know the subject to be discussed (maybe some of the other guys there didn't know, either!) but we'd felt led to tape it.

Brother Bill laid it on the line regarding the duties of a husband. His instructions really impressed me. So here, with his permission, I'm going to quote part of what he told us husbands as he emphasized that the husband is to love the wife.

> You'll talk to an old boy and he'll say, "She knows I love her."
> 
> "Really?"
> 
> "Yeah. I told her a couple of anniversaries ago. She knows it. Man, she gets my paycheck every Friday. I sign it and she buys the food, clothes for the kids, makes a car payment and a TV payment. I'm here every night. She knows I love her."
> 
> That's garbage. That's the devil's rubbish.
> 
> I don't care how many times you've said it, under what conditions you've said it, *you tell your wife you love her.*

I don't care when it is, how it is, you let her know *verbally* that you love her.

Don't ever rely on the fact that you do a good hard day's work at the office and then come home. Tell her. Let her know. You're not trying to con her or build her up or make her something she's not—but if you love your wife, tell her so.

So many men cop out by saying, "It's so hard to put in words how I feel." That's hogwash. You put into words how you feel about everything else!

Husbands, love your wives. God wants you to love your wife because she is a woman; and God made woman with a need and a capacity for love.

Man, if you don't know that right now you'd better wake up. The reason that crowd's running around with the Women's Lib business today is they've not lived in an environment of love.

The greatest thing a daddy can do for his children is to love their mother. For your child to see and to know, "My daddy loves my mother," is the greatest strength and security you can provide. Teach him how to love, to share your love, to return it, to respond. All this must be taught by example.

The Bible says you're to love your wife *as Christ loved the church*. That's a big order. That's selfless love. It's also completeness—no partial love, no fragments. He gave Himself totally and completely.

In Ephesians 5:28, "So ought men to love their wives as their own bodies . . . ." Right. Jesus said, "Thy twain shall be one flesh . . ." [Mark 10:8].

No man is complete in the fullness and intent of God unless he has a wife. He simply hasn't got all God would like for him to have. God's mathematics says, one plus one equals—one. And man's love for his wife is to be complete, total, and without reservation.

In Ephesians 5:21, Paul tells us we are to submit ourselves one to another in the fear of God. That's husbands and wives. The next verse says, "Wives, submit yourselves unto your own husbands, as unto the Lord." That means in all things, leaving nothing out.

The husband is to be all-giving. The wife is to be totally submissive in all things. There they are, both submitting themselves, both giving totally. That's Christian marriage.

The husband does not dominate, but he knows she is made to receive his love, and if she does not receive that love, she will not receive.

When the husband is giving, and the wife giving, both are receiving *only* what they can receive when both are giving.

God instituted two things; the family and the church. Anytime people monkey with God's institutions, they get hurt. God wants only the very best for us. He has put marriage and family in the Scripture, and told us how to model these holy institutions.

Meanwhile, men, there's a tremendous responsibility you and I will face at the judgment seat of Christ—as the head of the wife.

That's Brother Bill for you. His admonitions come straight from the Bible. No matter how you live at home—no matter how you act toward your wife—you can't argue with him—because he's right.

When you apply God's standards as to how you love your wife, you begin to mature—no more games. I think there has been a minimum amount of maneuvering so far as Anita and I are concerned. I don't ever try to put things over on her. I can't remember ever seriously trying to fool her, except maybe with a birthday surprise—that kind of thing.

But my sarcasm has hurt Anita. It really cuts her. Obviously I've got to mature past that!

Sometimes I think I'm the only one who ever comes out

and disagrees with Anita Bryant. *In the whole world!* I get tired of it occasionally—the repercussions. But if she didn't have one person who disagreed with her, it would be disastrous for her. I can't think of anyone else who gives her a hard time.

I know I'm important to Anita—how lonely it is, not having people tell you how it really is and what you really are.

She trusts me.

"Husbands, love your wives." When I look back at our early years, with their lack of spiritual content, I can hardly compare them to what we know now. Still, even at our worst, we had what I consider a normal family structure: man, wife, children. Nowadays in this world, roles seem to get terribly confused.

"The Bible teaches that the man is to be primarily the breadwinner, his wife, primarily the mother and homemaker," Brother Bill said. "These are fulltime jobs.

"The mother in our society has always had a special place. The wife of the husband is the mother of the children. Because of that, she is queen of the home. As for the role of mother, there's no other responsibility like it on the face of this earth."

As Anita and I travel about the country, we can't help but believe the sexes are getting closer together. There's not as much difference between boys and girls as there used to be.

Many young men today seem to have abandoned the male role. They refuse to be heads of households. I don't think a serious young woman should marry someone like that because I don't think she's going to change him.

It's frightening. I don't know if physical appearance or mode of attire or these things make the difference, but it seems guys are more docile. They're almost feminine in manner and dress, and their attitudes toward girls are very lackadaisical and ungallant.

A good many girls these days assume the male role and call boys for dates. I have a nagging feeling that boys are going to get less and less interested in girls as a result.

The intrigue is going. If a girl wants to put herself on an equal plane with the boy, she's going to find herself less and less in demand. It used to be that if guys wanted to date a sharp girl they had to polish the car and fix themselves up—and compete. If they don't have to do that, they're going to lose interest.

Maybe girls phone boys from necessity. Maybe the boys don't have that get-up-and-go—that desire. I see an extreme lack of desire in young men today.

They get married, and then there are no clear-cut role definitions. Furthermore their children—even babies—run loose. They just don't seem to care what happens to their children.

In order to curb these trends, we must get back to the Bible. We need to start our children out with God's Word which provides the only authoritative role definition for man, woman, husband, wife, or child.

I'm saying we've got to go back to the basic, old-fashioned family structure, or have chaos in this country. Unless you have discipline, beginning with the head of the house and continuing through every member, we're going to see the days of Rome all over again.

I really fear this country could cease to exist. We're rearing weak children. Where you have a bunch of weak males, everything is going to cave in. Women are getting stronger and men weaker.

And that brings us back to where we began—with the role of the Christian husband. He *must* assume the leadership of his home because God has told him to.

"Anything that has two heads is a freak of nature," Brother Bill told us. "The woman is to allow the man, through her submission, to be head of the home, as Christ is head of the church.

"The man must be first and foremost the breadwinner. The woman must be mother and homemaker. If one of them fails these duties, man or wife, they cannot get done. If we renege on our responsibility, we lose."

This is too much to lose.

Chapter 5 of Ephesians puts it on the line for Christian husbands and wives—children, too.

"Marriage has never been 50–50," Brother Bill said. "It has always been—if it's God-honoring—100–100. Total loving, yielding, giving—100 percent, *100 percent!*"

That's talking about marriage in the Lord.

The Bible says, "Husbands, love your wives." And nowhere does it tell you where to draw the line—where to stop!

# *14*

# *Bless This House*

*So much has happened since Bob and I wrote the first few pages of this book together. We knew from the outset we'd call it "Bless This House" but we couldn't have known Villa Verde, our house, literally was to be blessed by evangelist Billy Graham.*

*We saved this story for last, because it involves your family —and your house, too.*

Meanwhile, coincidentally, Chuck Bird wrote a song for Anita called "God Bless This House." Maybe the book had something to do with it—I don't know.

The song is a bell-ringer—the first sacred thing Chuck has written, I believe. Anita likes it so well she made it the title song of a new album which will come out about the same

time as this book—the book we didn't have time to write—
the record she didn't have time to cut!

*Chuck is our conductor-arranger, of course. The lyrics of
his new song are beautiful, conveying the idea not only of a
house, but also of one's body as being the house of God. He
became inspired to write this song in the middle of the night.
He jumped out of bed and wrote the lyrics at three o'clock
in the morning.*

*It's an unusual, moving composition. There are several
verses. Bob and I want to share with you a portion of the
lyrics:*

> This house You built in which to dwell,
>    without You is an empty shell.
>
> As dark and lonesome as a tomb,
>    please God be in my every room.
>
> The welcome mat is at my door,
>    no one could love You any more.
>
> And in Your hand You hold the key,
>    for all who want eternity.
>
> I pray to You—GOD BLESS THIS HOUSE.

Words and Music by
CHUCK BIRD

And now it's Good Friday, 1972. It's a very special day
for our family because Billy Graham and Grady Wilson, his
Crusades' associate, visited us at Villa Verde. Billy had come
to Miami Beach to preach the Easter sunrise services at
Miami Marine Stadium.

Last summer, Anita and I enjoyed having lunch and spending the afternoon with Billy and Ruth Graham at their mountaintop home in Montreat, North Carolina. It really was a rare occasion for us.

That day it struck me how much Billy Graham, the most far-ranging evangelist the world has ever known, hungers and thirsts to hear about people who have come to the Lord. Anita and I sat with the Grahams and shared some of the wonderful things the Lord has done for us. We spoke of our first attempts at witnessing for Christ. Billy listened as though he'd never heard such fascinating stories before.

It made us love him all the more, realizing that with him, each conversion story is a separate, brand-new miracle. And of course it really is.

*I loved Ruth Graham, who is exactly the kind of woman I would like to be. I like to hear Billy talk about her. He says Ruth is so fearless she'll chase a rattlesnake down the trail, grab it by the tail, give a snap and break its neck. Billy says she's not afraid of anything.*

*News that Billy and Grady were coming really galvanized our household. As any woman would, I whirled in and did a big spring housecleaning. Everybody was excited around here.*

*Fredda Walker, our friend from church, came in to help make the big day run smoothly. "I could never get excited and interested in other celebrities, but Billy Graham is a man of God," she said.*

*Martha Mayes, our housekeeper of the past seven years, pretty well ran the show, and Susie Evans, new to our household, assisted. Linda Carver, sometime secretary and a member of our church, helped with baby-sitting. And Jody*

*Dunton, the expert nurse of premature babies who is our twins' sweet friend as well as ours, took care of them. Jody has loved them since she met them at Jackson Memorial Hospital, and we've loved her since then.*

We asked Linda if she'd be excited to meet Billy Graham, and she said something pretty wonderful. "Yes—not just because he's one of the best-loved men in the world, and one of the most famous men in history—but because of the Christ in him."

Our teen-age friends are something special. Kathie Epstein had to be in Chicago for an appearance. Michele, her sister, was coming here for Easter holidays. Billy Graham is their hero, but they never have met him. They were longing to be here with us. However, they'd made a commitment to sing at a small church in Indiantown, Florida, so they kept their appointment.

*These girls have so much Christian character. Bob and I really enjoy them. For my birthday, Diane Graham, our pianist at Northwest Baptist Church, wrote me a card which read:*

HAPPY BIRTHDAY, ANITA. YOU HAVE EVERYTHING, SO I'M GIVING YOU ME. HERE ARE EIGHT BABY-SITTING NIGHTS, ABSO-LUTELY FREE. LOVE IN JESUS, DI-DI.

*Kathie Epstein also created a very personal gift, a hand-made notebook in which to put names of people I'm espe-cially praying for. She covered it in a beautiful crewel work she designed and stitched, and she composed a poem for me:*

To Anita:
May the Lord always bless you with beauty and health,
And always supply you with heavenly wealth.
May you always seek Jesus in all that you do,
That the world may see Him when they look at you.
May you always have wisdom in earthly affairs,
That your life may be free of burdens and cares.
May you always be praising with each note you sing,
The Saviour who blessed you with everything.
And friend, may you always have peace in your soul,
A gift from the Healer who mends and makes whole.

Lovingly and eternally,

KAFFEY-CAKE

Billy and Grady arrived about 4:30 in the afternoon. Not only was it Good Friday, but Anita remembered still another significant thing about the day: It was exactly four years ago on Good Friday that we moved into Villa Verde.

"Isn't that great?" she said. "Bob, what if we asked Billy to bless this house. You know—to say some kind of special, private, formal kind of blessing."

Then we both stared at one another. I guess we had the same thought at the same time.

*Billy came "formal," dressed up in shirt and tie. Grady arrived in an orange-and-brown print shirt, sporting a blue baseball cap, and I told him he looked like a sure 'nuff tourist. He'd bought Billy a real flamboyant purple print shirt. I told Billy to go put it on.*

*"Take off your undershirt so you won't be too hot," I suggested.*

*"Quit bossing him around like you do me!" Bob said.*

*(I think Bob was a little horrified. Well, I don't know whether he took it off or not!)*

Pedro and I put the lighted cross on the roof, the cross we always put up at Christmas. Billy and Grady liked that.

We took them on a tour of the house before dinner, and when Billy saw our family's altar he said he'd only seen a couple of others like it—in England. He'd never before seen one in the United States.

*As I said before, I'm a big admirer of Ruth Bell Graham. Months ago, one of the women's magazines interviewed me as part of a feature they ran. They wanted to know the names of the two women I most admired. I named Catherine Marshall and Ruth Graham.*

*When I popped into a drugstore to buy a copy of the magazine, curious to see the article, I discovered it was selling like hot cakes. The reason? That issue had a picture of a nude male in the centerfold!*

*Well, it had other pictures more interesting. One was Ruth Graham's, and I showed it to Billy. Later, when he phoned Ruth at home in Montreat, he couldn't resist kidding her.*

*"Hey honey," he said, "Your picture is in a magazine this month, along with a nude man in the centerfold."*

We had a real family dinner. We fixed steaks and ate outside in the gallery, all very relaxed despite the rain. At the table were Jody Dunton, Grady Wilson, Billy Graham,

Anita, myself and our children Bobby, Gloria, Billy and Barbara.

We had talked about Easter all week long. All the children know about Christ's crucifixion and resurrection—even the twins. They were sitting at the table in their high chairs, and I said to our little Billy, very casually: "Tell our guests what Easter is all about."

His eyes sparkled. He broke into a big grin.

"Easter is the black bunny taking all the eggs from the white bunny," he said, much to my embarrassment. (He got that from television, as you might guess.) That should teach me! Kids never come through when you're trying to show them off.

*Almost as soon as Billy Graham arrived, I popped the question. Bob and I told him right away about this book, and he seemed very interested in it.*

*"Also, Billy, this is our fourth anniversary in this house," I told him. "And it never has been blessed. I mean—you know—had a blessing said over it. Could you . . . ?"*

*"Of course," he said, smiling. "That's a wonderful idea."*

*"But Billy, we didn't mean just for us. How about if Bob turned on the tape recorder, and we took it down word for word. We'd like to put your blessing in our book. We'd like other Christians to use it as a prayer to bless their homes, if they'd like."*

*"Hey, that's great!" he said.*

Billy blessed the house as his grace before dinner. I did set up the tape recorder, and I think we were all very pleased and excited about what was happening. Even the children understood.

After dinner a few other guests came in for some great fellowship. Brother Bill Chapman arrived with his wife Peggy. Charlie and Marabel Morgan came, and so did Renny and Janet Berry. Charlie Walker, Fredda's husband, came to pick her up, but we asked him to join us instead.

Conversation flowed easily. Mostly we shared Christian experiences, all very easygoing and low-key, the kind of fellowship you'd find in a group of like-believers anywhere.

Sometimes people ask Anita and me what Billy Graham is really like. "Is he like he is on television?"

That's a tough one. He's just Billy—natural, unassuming, completely down-to-earth. One of the best-loved men in the history of the world, yet humble. He has no pretenses whatever.

Watching our group, I found myself thinking who I'd like to emulate. Anita and I have met many celebrities. We have slept at the White House, visited with presidents and high-ranking foreign dignitaries, met people important in American business, government, and the entertainment world. We have had some interesting experiences with unusual people.

And whom do I most admire?

Charlie Walker for one, I decided. It occurred to me I wouldn't want to be anybody famous or well known, anybody you ever heard of. I'd not trade places with anybody, actually, but I do sort of envy a few people.

Charlie Walker, Fredda's husband, is a mechanic for National Air Lines. After work he spends hours each week servicing and driving our church busses from which the church conducts one of its most important ministries.

And I thought about Brother Virgil Pool, my former Sunday-school teacher who once did something I greatly admired. He went before our congregation and publicly confessed a sin which had burdened him for a long time. It was probably nothing anybody knew about—just that he'd had bad feelings toward Brother Bill when he first became our pastor.

Brother Pool prayed about this and eventually changed toward Brother Bill. He wanted to bring it before the congregation and confess it. To me, that represented complete submission to the Lord—real freedom and honesty.

I think the average person is too phony to expose his ugly places to others. But I'm seeing more and more clearly that Christians have a rapport other people just don't have.

I looked around the room filled with our Christian friends —the salt of the earth. I felt very grateful. What kind of men do I admire? Not celebrities or men the world considers especially successful. But Virgil Pool, Charlie Walker. They represent the kind of man I want to become.

*I looked around the room too, with great gratitude to God. The Holy Spirit came among us as we shared. The love and tenderness in our fellowship was something to be cherished forever in our memories. It was a very special Good Friday.*

*Our group represented many ages (from toddlers to those in middle years), but it struck me how little difference this makes. Each of us is Christian—each in his own stage of Christian growth. Ministers and babies and housewives—all of us have dedicated our lives to Christ.*

*My mind also wandered a little. I thought of the morning Kathy Miller, my Sunday-school teacher, announced she'd have to be out of town a couple of weeks. She asked if anyone felt led to teach the class. I felt as though she were looking right at me. Suddenly I had the desire to do this.*

*"I'll take one of the Sundays," I offered.*

*"Praise the Lord. We've been praying for that," she said.*

*Later I wondered why I'd offered because the devil started working overtime on me. The only time I could find to study seemed to be late at night after everyone else was in bed. I was up until midnight all that week, studying.*

*Kathie Epstein made some posters for me. I worked so hard that week at my text, James 1:12–15. I really began to appreciate how much effort and time Bob puts into his classes.*

*I respect him and look up to him for this. Just that one week was a hardship for me, so I began to get some glimmer of the dedication other Christians have toward advancing and teaching the Word of God.*

*Oh yes, the Holy Spirit was with me that morning I taught. My knees shook, but we got through it. I learned much more from the Bible knowing I was going to get up there before those gals on Sunday morning—and had to be able to answer their sincere questions.*

*My eyes circled the room again. I was seeing our friends in terms of their Christian service, their devotion, their selflessness, and I was loving them. I want to become that kind of Christian.*

As people shared, the power of witnessing continued to hit me. We didn't know, for example, that Jody Dunton had been saved on Anita's birthday, back in 1961, at a Billy Graham Crusade.

We did know our little Kathie Epstein's mother had come to Christ through one of Billy's Crusades some years ago. Later Kathie's father was saved, and their girls subsequently were reared as staunch little believers.

Anita and I look at these teen-agers, so strong in the faith, and get an idea of what we can expect of ours in a few years.

And the Christian life all begins with somebody's testimony.

*Just before our evening had to end, we all joined hands in a circle and Billy Graham said a prayer. We'd had a thundershower that hot afternoon, and now the breeze blew cool among us. It had been a beautiful Good Friday.*

*"Thank God on this Good Friday for fellowship with those of us who have personal relationships to Him," Billy prayed. We all felt very close to one another.*

*Billy autographed our Bibles for the entire Green clan. I pinned a gold fish hook on his lapel and one on Grady Wilson's. And Bob and I thanked Billy again for blessing our house.*

*Billy's prayer is simple, unpretentious, and somehow sounds very American. We hope you like it too, and use it to bless your house as a home committed to Christ.*

*Our Father, we thank Thee for all the blessings we have every day; the material things that Thou dost give us, and the spiritual things Thou dost give us.*

*Thou hast said that except the* Lord *build a house, they labor in vain that build. We thank Thee that in* this *house Thou hast had a great part in building it; in building a marriage, building a family, building a career, and in building a home.*

*We thank Thee for the sense of Thy Presence we feel in this home, and we pray it will always be here.*

*We pray that this house will always glorify Jesus Christ.*

*We thank Thee for this food and this fellowship, in Christ's name. Amen.*

BILLY GRAHAM
Villa Verde
Good Friday
March 31, 1972